VALHALLA

BY PAUL MURPHY

Valhalla won the Theatre503 Playwriting Award 2014, and was developed
and produced by Theatre503 in association with Sheer Drop Theatre

It received its world premiere at Theatre503 on
Wednesday 30 September 2015

VALHALLA
BY PAUL MURPHY

CAST

Man	Clint Dyer
Woman	Carolina Main

CREATIVE TEAM

Director	Jo McInnes
Designer	Katie Lias
Lighting Designer	Nigel Edwards
Sound Designer	Becky Smith
Casting Director	Matthew Dewsbury
Assistant Director	Tom Latter
Video Designers	Dominic Baker, Oliver Levett
Costume Supervisor	Freyja Costelloe
Prop Maker	Alice Amesbury

PRODUCTION TEAM

Producer	Jessica Campbell
General Manager	Jeremy Woodhouse
Associate Producer	Franky Green
Production Manager	Heather Doole
Stage Manager	Martha Mamo
Production PR	Chloe Nelkin Consulting
Resident Assistant Producers	Ceri Lothian and Scott Barnett

CAST

CLINT DYER (Man)

Recent theatre includes: *The New Order* (writer/actor, The Big Idea, Royal Court); *The Royale, Perseverance Drive, A Carpet, A Pony and a Monkey* (Bush); *Sus* (Young Vic/tour); *Michael X* (Eclipse/The Tabernacle); *Big White Fog* (Almeida); *Sus* (Stratford East at Greenwich); *Skaville* (Soho).

Recent film includes: *Mine* (forthcoming: dir. Fabio & Fabio for the Safran Co); *Montana* (dir. Mo Ali for Moli Films); *Arthur Christmas* (dir. Sarah Smith & Barry Cook for Aardman); *Unknown* (dir. Jaume Collet-Serra for Warners); *Sus* (dir. Rob Heath for 3rd Eye Film); *Agora* (dir. Alejandro Amenabar for Mod Producciones); *Mr Bean's Holiday* (dir. Steve Bendelack for Working Title); *Portrait of London* (dir. Simon McBurny/Mike Figgis); *The Trail* (dir. Eric Valli); *Sahara* (dir. Breck Eisner, for Paramount); *Out on a Limb* (dir. Rob Heath); *Cherps* (dir. Kolton Lee for Prophet Pictures); *Mr Inbetween* (dir. Paul Sarrossy for Lionsgate).

Television credits include: *Hope Springs* (Series Reg – Shed Productions); *Fallout* (Company Pictures); *MI High* (Kudos Productions); *Trial and Retribution XII* (LaPlante Productions); *Dalziel and Pascoe* (BBC); *Inspector Lynley* (BBC); *The Commander* (LaPlante Productions); *'Orrible* (BBC); *Homie and Away* (Shona Productions); *Skank* (BBC/Shona); *Douglas* (BBC); *Thief Takers* (Central) and *Prime Suspect* (Granada).

Awards include: for *Sus* – Screen Nation (Best Actor), Liege Film Festival (Best Actor), Texas Black Film Festival (Best Actor); he also has two Best Actor nominations from BFM International Film Festival and the British Urban Film Festival.

CAROLINA MAIN (Woman)

Carolina recently appeared in *Grantchester* (ITV, dir: Harry Bradbeer); *Old Jack's Boat* (CBBC) and *Borgia III* (Film United, dir: Athina Tsangari).

Theatre credits include: *King Lear* (RSC, dir: Tim Crouch) and *The Winter's Tale* and *All's Well That Ends Well* (Cambridge Shakespeare Festival).

Short film includes: *The Swimmer* (Warp Films, dir: Lynne Ramsay).

CREATIVES

PAUL MURPHY (Writer)
Paul is a London-based playwright. He was the joint winner of Theatre503's inaugural Playwriting Award in 2014. *Valhalla* is his full-length professional debut.

JO MCINNES (Director)
Jo is Associate Director of the Hackney Showroom and Artistic Director of the Hackney Showroom's resident theatre company mobculture which she co-founded in 2013. In 2006 Jo held the position of Artistic Director of New Writing South and she has directed workshops and rehearsed readings of new work for, amongst others, the Royal Court Theatre, the Old Vic and Hampstead Theatre. Jo is currently working on an operatic version of Sarah Kane's *4.48 Psychosis* with the composer Philip Venables. She has also worked extensively as an actor.

Recent directing work includes: *36 Phone Calls* (Hampstead); *Another Place* (Theatre Royal Plymouth); *I Can Hear You & This Is Not An Exit* (Midsummer Mischief Season, RSC Stratford/Royal Court); *Carpe Diem* (New Views/ National Theatre); *Vera, Vera, Vera, Red Bud* (Royal Court); *Marine Parade* (Animalink/Brighton Festival) and *Christmas* (Brighton/Bush).

KATIE LIAS (Designer)
Katie studied English Literature and Theatre at Royal Holloway University, before specialising in Set and Costume Design at RADA. Upon graduating, she worked as a Resident Design Assistant at the Royal Shakespeare Company (2008–2009).

Recent theatre credits include: *The Lone Pine Club* (Pentabus); *Journey's End* (Watermill); *Dick Whittington, Cinderella* (costumes, Lyric Hammersmith); *Nanny McPhee* (costumes, Peacock Theatre/London Children's Ballet); *Address Unknown* (Soho); *Lee Harvey Oswald* (Finborough); *In the Summer House, Penthisilea, Man Equals Man* (RADA); *Alice's Adventures in Wonderland* (costumes), *Grandad, Me and Teddy Too* (Polka); *The Welsh Boy, Deadkindssongs* (costumes, Ustinov Theatre Royal Bath); *The Addams Family Musical, Antigone, Love and Information, Love and Money, Ice Cream, Liliom, On The Razzle* (Arts Ed); *Coalition, Word: Play 3* (Theatre503); *Much Ado About Nothing* (East 15); *Tinderbox* (Tooting Arts Club); *The Tempest* (RSC tour); *The Fred Karno Project* (Bristol Old Vic); *The Lower Depths* (Baron's Court); *No Expense Spared* (Jermyn Street); *The Plague* (Lost); *The Day They Banned Christmas* (Courtyard).

NIGEL EDWARDS (Lighting Designer)

In Britain, Nigel is best known as the lighting designer for Forced Entertainment, designing twenty-six of their shows since 1990. Other shows of interest include *Lanark* (Citizens); the premieres of Sarah Kane's *Cleansed* and *448 Psychosis* (Royal Court); *Crave* (Paines Plough); *Roberto Zucco, The Mysteries, Victoria, The Tempest* and *Troilus and Cressida* (with the Wooster Group, RSC); Debbie Tucker Green's *Dirty Butterfly* and *Trade* (Soho); and *Stoning Mary* (Royal Court).

Dance credits include: *50 Acts, Dance Dance Dance, Desert Island Dances, Pigg in Hell, Total Masala Slammer, The HCA project, Solo* and *Portraits Berlin*.

West End credits include: *Sexual Perversity in Chicago, When Harry Met Sally* and *The Postman Always Rings Twice*.

Opera credits include: *Jenufa* (WNO); *The Maids* (ENO) and *Hansel and Gretel* (Opera North).

Nigel is the lighting designer for Ryuichi Sakamoto and has designed and toured with Jeff Beck Diamanda Galas Carsten Nicolai, Yellow Magic Orchestra, Ólafur Arnalds and Joss Pook.

BECKY SMITH (Sound Designer)

Becky studied drama at Exeter University.

Sound designs include: *Joanne* (Latitude Festival); *36 Phonecalls* (Hampstead Theatre); *The Day After* (Vault Festival); *Bird* (Derby Playhouse); *Little on the Inside* (Summerhall, Edinburgh); *Circles, Frozen* (Birmingham Rep); *Billy the Girl* (Soho); *The Only Way is Chelsea's* (York Theatre Royal); *The Kitchen Sink* (Hull Truck); *The Well and the Badly Loved, Lagan* (Ovalhouse); *Cardboard Dad* (Sherman Cymru); *It felt empty…* (Space K, Arcola); *This Wide Night* (Soho); *Brood* (Stratford East); *The Juniper Tree* (UK tour); *Reverence* (Southwark Playhouse), *The Ghost Sonata* (Trinity Buoy Wharf).

Becky also freelances in Radio Drama for the BBC.

MATTHEW DEWSBURY (Casting Director)

Matthew is the Casting Assistant at the Royal Shakespeare Company. Prior to that he was the Casting and Producing Assistant at the Watermill Theatre.

Credits as Casting Director include: *And Then Come The Nightjars, Animals* and *A Handful of Stars* (Theatre503/Trafalgar Studios, West End transfer), all for Theatre503; *A Mad World, My Masters,* RSC/ETT; *Little Malcolm and his Struggle against the Eunuchs* (Soggy Arts at Southwark Playhouse); *The Late Henry Moss* (W14 Productions at Southwark Playhouse); *Much Ado About Nothing* (Reading Between the Lines); *Ragnorak* (Eastern Angles); *Glamping (Now I am Running Stag)* (Windswept Productions; workshop).

TOM LATTER (Assistant Director)
Tom trained in Directing at Mountview Academy and works as a director and dramaturg.

Theatre credits as director include: *Dirty Promises* (Hope Theatre – nominated for Best Director, Off West End Awards); *The Comedy of Errors* (The Space); *Beethoven's Always Right* and *Never Rains but it Pours* (Theatre503); *The Stolen Inches* (New Diorama); *The Death of Norman Tortilla* (Tristan Bates); *Plays What Yew Wrote* and *Lost and Found* (Saffron Walden Maze Festival).

As Assistant Director: *Our Ajax* by Timberlake Wertenbaker, directed by David Mercatali (Southwark Playhouse).

Tom is the Literary Coordinator at Theatre503 and Artistic Director of Sheer Drop Theatre.

HEATHER DOOLE (Production Manager)
Heather is a freelance production manager. She has previously worked at Theatre503 on *Cinderella and the Beanstalk*, *Animals* and *And Then Come The Nightjars*.

Other credits include: *State Red, Elephants, Deposit, Deluge, Sunspots* and *36 Phone Calls* (all Hampstead Theatre Studio); *Radiant Vermin* (Soho/Tobacco Factory, Bristol); *Albert Herring* (Upstairs at the Gatehouse). She assisted on *Bull* (Young Vic).

MARTHA MAMO (Stage Manager)
Martha trained at The Royal Welsh College of Music and Drama.

Theatre credits include: *Running Wild, Way Upstream* (Chichester Festival Theatre); *The Shoemaker's Holiday, Midsummer Mischief Festival, Antony and Cleopatra, Boris Godunov, The Heresy of Love, Measure for Measure* (RSC); *Neighbors* (HighTide); *Egusi Soup* (Menagerie); *Realism, Mongrel Island* (Soho); *Ivan and the Dogs* (ATC); *Light Shining on Buckinghamshire, The Painter* (Arcola); *Kursk* (Fuel/Sound and Fury); *Breathing Irregular, The Kreutzer Sonarta* (Gate); *The Pride, A Miracle, The Peckham Soap Opera* (Royal Court); *Parade* (Donmar Warehouse); *Julius Caesar* (BITE); *The Bull, Flower Bed* (Fabulous Beast); *The Changeling* (Cheek By Jowl).

JESSICA CAMPBELL (Producer)

Jessica is the Producer and Head of Marketing at Theatre503.

Producing credits include: *Green Living* and *Four Play* (rehearsed readings for the Old Vic); *How I Learned To Drive* and *A Bright Room Called Day* (Southwark Playhouse); *Sense of an Ending* and *First World Problem* (Theatre503); *Stink Foot* (Yard Theatre); *Tango* (rehearsed reading for the Young Vic); *Hansel and Gretel* (Bussey Building); *Mephisto* (Oxford Playhouse) and a UK/Japan tour of *The Comedy of Errors* (Southwark Playhouse, Yvonne Arnaud Theatre, Stratford's The Dell, Hatfield House and Tokyo Metropolitan Theatre.)

FRANKY GREEN (Associate Producer)

Franky is a freelance theatre producer. She graduated from the BA Drama Course at Bristol University in 2014 and was a Resident Assistant Producer at Theatre503 from December 2014–June 2015. She is currently an Associate Producer for two theatre companies, Bellow Theatre and Tap Tap Theatre.

Producing credits include: *And Then Come The Nightjars* (Theatre503); *Billy Through the Window* (Underbelly, Edinburgh Festival/Theatre503 preview); *Captain Morgan and the Sands of Time* (VAULT Festival); *Handmade Tales* (Arcola/London Wonderground Festival/ZOO, Edinburgh Festival); *Men* (Arcola/Underbelly, Edinburgh Festival); *Beautiful Thing* and *Low Tide in Glass Bay* (Alma Tavern Theatre, Bristol); *Breathing Corpses* (White Theatre, Bristol), *The Tempest* and *Trash* (Winston Theatre, Bristol).

Particular thanks to

Abbie McCamley
Amber Hockridge
Amy Dier
Annie Eves
Bethany Reilly
Carla Smith
Dewi Sarginson
Ebony Wong
Elham Mahyoub
Eva Bradley-Williams
Evie Osbon
Gaby French
Gemma Kenny
Halema Hussain
Harriet Grenville
Isabella McGough
Jane Cottrell
Kelly Blackburn
Lauren Bradshaw
Lucinda Jarvis
Nicole Bartlett
Raphaelle Collou
Rosemary Berkon
Sarah Balfour

This production has been supported by:

Thanks

Academy of Live and Recorded Arts
Adam Loxley
Aly Spiro at ALRA
Annabel Winder at ETT
Annie Brewer at Jerwood Space
Austin Spangler
Ben Hall
Bishanyia Vincent
Chris Campbell
Clemmie Medforth
Central School of Speech and Drama
Corinne Salisbury
Deborah Bowman
Dennis Kelly
Diana Moss & Mark Gubbins
Eleanor Lloyd
English Touring Theatre
Erica Whyman
George Linfield
Geraldine Sharpe-Newton
Giles Gartrell-Mills
Henry Hitchings
Ian Sims
Jack Sain
Jack Tilbury

James & Meg Stewart
Jerwood Space
Jo Hedley
John Bowis
Kay Ellen Consolver
Lily Williams
Marcus Markou
Margret Kristin Sigurdardottir
Marianne Elliot
Michael Davenport
Michael Ross
Morag Sims
Neil Darlison at Arts Council England
Nessa Carey
Penelope Sheffield Sims
Peter Smith
Philip and Chris Carne
Polly Ingham
Robert Bradley
Royce Bell
Roy Williams
Saul Reid
Tanya Ronder
Yasmin Joseph

Thanks to the Theatre503 script readers:
Anna Landi, Anna Mors, Ben Hall, Bobby Brook, Brett Westwell, Bridget Hanley, Carla Grauls, Carla Kingham, Claire O'Hara, Corinne Salisbury, Deborah Nash, Deirdre O'Halloran, Jill Segal, Joel Ormsby, Kate Brower, Lisa Carroll, Martin Edwards, Micha Colombo, Sarah Newton, Saul Reid, Tamsin Irwin, Tim Lee, Tom Littler, Tommo Fowler, Vinay Patel, Yasmeen Arden, Catherine Marcus, Kat Andrews, Imogen Sarre, Kealey Ridgen, Kim Marchant, Martha Cooke, Megan Phillips, Sara Gad, Steve Harvey and Zandra Israel

THEATRE503

Theatre503 is the award-winning home of groundbreaking plays.

Led by Artistic Director Paul Robinson, Theatre503 is a flagship fringe venue committed to producing new work that is game-changing, relevant, surprising, mischievous, visually thrilling and theatrical. We are the smallest theatre to win an Olivier award and we offer more opportunities to new writers than anywhere in the UK.

THEATRE503 TEAM

Artistic Director	Paul Robinson
Executive Director	Jeremy Woodhouse
Producer and Head of Marketing	Jessica Campbell
Associate Artistic Director	Lisa Cagnacci
Literary Manager	Steve Harper
Literary Coordinators	Lauretta Barrow, Tom Latter
Office Manager	Anna De Freitas
Resident Assistant Producers	Ceri Lothian, Scott Barnett
'Young Creative Leaders' Project Manager	Louise Abbotts
Volunteer Coordinators	Serafina Cusack, Simon Mander
Associate Directors	Anna Jordan, Jonathan O'Boyle
Senior Readers	Karis Halsall, Kate Brower, Clare O'Hara, Jimmy Osborne, Imogen Sarre

THEATRE503 BOARD

Royce Bell, Peter Benson, Chris Campbell, Kay Ellen Consolver, Ben Hall, Dennis Kelly, Eleanor Lloyd, Marcus Markou, Geraldine Sharpe-Newton, Jack Tilbury, Erica Whyman (Chair), Roy Williams.

We couldn't do what we do without our volunteers:
Andrei Vornicu, Annabel Pemberton Bethany Doherty, Charlotte Mulliner, Chidi Chukwu, Damian Robertson, Danielle Wilson, Fabienne Gould, George Linfield, James Hansen, Joanna Lallay, Kelly Agredo, Ken Hawes, Larner Taylor, Mandy Nicholls, Mark Doherty, Mike Murgaz, Nicole Marie, Rahim Dhanji, Rosie Akerman, Tess Hardy.

Theatre503 is supported by:
Philip and Chris Carne, Cas Donald, Gregory Dunlop, Angela Hyde-Courtney and the Audience Club, Stephanie Knauf, Sumintra Latchman, Katherine Malcolm, Georgia Oetker, Francesca Ortona, Geraldine Sharpe-Newton.

Support Theatre503
Help us take risks on new writers and produce the plays other theatres can't, or won't. Together we can discover the writers of tomorrow and make some of the most exciting theatre in the country. With memberships ranging from £23 to £1003 there is a chance to get involved no matter what your budget, to help us remain *'arguably the most important theatre in Britain today'* (*Guardian*)

Benefits range from priority notice of our work and news, access to sold out shoes, ticket deals, and opportunities to attend parties and peek into rehearsals. Visit theatre503.com or call 020 7978 7040 for more details.

Theatre503, 503 Battersea Park Rd, London SW11 3BW
020 7978 7040 | www.theatre503.com
@Theatre503 | Facebook.com/theatre503

Sheer Drop Theatre develops and stages the work of new and emerging playwrights of any age. Working with writers to develop plays through script-reading and dramaturgy, workshop processes, rehearsed readings and showings, we are committed to becoming a vital part of the whole country's theatrical seedbed.

Our particular passion is nurturing writers at the beginning of their careers to create the leading playwrights of the future. Of the ten plays we have produced to date, seven were the writer's first major production.

We are drawn to plays which explore the big issues of the day through human stories; drama that is thought-provoking and touching; plays which make you think, melt the heart and tickle the funny-bone all at once.

Praise for Sheer Drop's work

'Clever and powerful… too visceral to ignore – it's not like a lot of other theatre, but that's the beauty of new writing as good as this'
One Stop Arts on *The Death of Norman Tortilla* by Charlotte Coates, 2012

'A beautifully crafted story that will hit you hard and remain with you when the lights go up'
The Upcoming on *Dirty Promises* by Lilly Driscoll, 2014,
nominated for Off West End Awards 2014 – Best Director

Artistic Directors
Tom Latter & Morag Sims

www.sheerdroptheatre.co.uk
@sheer_drop

VALHALLA

Paul Murphy

Acknowledgements

I would like to thank the following;

The cast and production team of *Valhalla* and all at Theatre503.

The Richard Carne Trust.

To Michael, Craig, Sarah, Henry and Mel for their encouragement and support.

To everyone at The Globe Shop.

My agents at Alan Brodie Representation and all at NHB.

P.M.

'The human body is the best picture of the human soul.'
Ludwig Wittgenstein

4

Characters

MAN
WOMAN

Setting

Act One – The City
Afterwards – The Island

Note on Text

A forward slash (/) indicates interrupted speech.

This text went to press before the end of rehearsals and so may differ slightly from the play as performed.

ACT ONE

Midgard

Scene One

In the darkness, noises begin to filter through. Human speech, indistinct, fractured. Glass shatters, screams, crashes, a howl of pain. A fire breaks out, spreading rapidly, it swallows everything in an almighty conflagration. Lights up. The living room of a modern apartment. The WOMAN *is sat on the floor, newspapers strewn around her.*

Pause.

The MAN *enters.*

MAN. Hi.

> *Beat.*

> Sorry I'm late, trains were packed. What we need, is a nice virulent flu epidemic. (*Goes into the kitchen.*) Have you eaten? I'm starving.

> *Beat.*

> *He re-enters, he is drinking from a sports bottle.*

> Jesus I'm sore. Bruises, look. Be worse tomorrow.

WOMAN. I thought your class was on Tuesdays.

MAN. It is Tuesday. (*Drinks.*) God that's disgusting. I'm going to shower.

WOMAN. You got on the train without having a shower?

MAN. Not very sociable. (*Holds up the bottle.*) Forgot this. Twenty-minute window to absorb the protein. Want a taste?

> *She shakes her head.*

> Are you hungry?

> *Beat.*

How was your day?

She shrugs.

Have you been out? Are you going to get dressed or…?

WOMAN. I am dressed.

Beat.

It's comfortable.

MAN. You could come. I know I've said it before.

WOMAN. Yes.

MAN. They have classes…

WOMAN. I don't want…

MAN. Or you could work out on your own, swim, run.

WOMAN. No.

MAN. Okay. Fine. I just think… something. This isn't healthy.

He goes through the newspapers.

WOMAN. You buy a newspaper every day.

MAN. That's different.

WOMAN. Just leave them.

MAN. The TV, the radio, the internet.

WOMAN. How can you not care?

MAN. I do care. But right now I care more about you.

WOMAN. That's how it starts.

Blackout.

Scene Two

The WOMAN *is sat at the table eating. Takeaway bags, etc. The* MAN *comes in.*

MAN. So, you were hungry?

WOMAN. Sorry.

MAN. It's fine. How is it?

WOMAN. Try some of this. (*Picks up a piece of food.*)

MAN. What is it?

WOMAN. Close your eyes.

MAN. Come on…

WOMAN. Don't you trust me?

MAN. Mmm. Okay.

   He closes his eyes.

WOMAN. No looking.

MAN. Okay.

WOMAN. Open.

MAN. I'm allergic to mushrooms, remember.

WOMAN. Shush.

   She puts a piece of food in his mouth. He chews.

MAN. Mmm, that's good. That's really good.

WOMAN. You're not allergic to mushrooms.

MAN. I don't like them.

WOMAN. Are you tired?

MAN. No.

WOMAN. You shouldn't overdo it.

MAN. I don't.

WOMAN. You look good.

MAN. It's futile really. Man versus machine, man versus nature. Doesn't get easier.

WOMAN. Not that old.

MAN. No.

WOMAN. Do you want some dessert?

MAN. I can't.

WOMAN. Course you can.

MAN. I shouldn't.

WOMAN. I think you should.

MAN. I'll have to spend even longer at the gym.

WOMAN. I thought you liked going.

She exits.

(*Off.*) The park's open again. I walked through it.

She re-enters with desert.

MAN. We could go for a walk?

WOMAN. We've got dessert.

MAN. Not necessarily now.

WOMAN. It's late.

MAN. Still light.

WOMAN. Maybe.

MAN. Most of the shops have reopened. Waiters are out on the street trying to entice people in? Remember Bangkok?

WOMAN. I'm tired.

MAN. You probably feel lethargic because... /

WOMAN. I'm tired.

MAN. Have you thought about work?

WOMAN. Yes.

Beat.

MAN. I thought you'd want to get back /

WOMAN. Did you?

MAN. Aren't they short-staffed?

WOMAN. Is that what worries you?

MAN. I just meant /

WOMAN. They'll survive. I'll go back when I'm ready.

   Beat.

MAN. Okay. It's fine. Whatever you want.

   Blackout.

Scene Three

WOMAN. Fuck off. Just fuck off.

MAN. You lied to me.

WOMAN. Fuck you.

MAN. Can we please stop this.

WOMAN. I made a choice.

MAN. That's what I'm saying.

WOMAN. I decided.

MAN. You decided to hide things?

WOMAN. I wanted to feel better.

MAN. Is this better?

WOMAN. This is about you.

MAN. No, it's about you.

WOMAN. Then you have nothing to say.

MAN. What about professional conduct?

WOMAN. What about it?

MAN. There are rules. There are guidelines.

WOMAN. Excuse me?

MAN. There's protocol.

WOMAN. Are you accusing me...

MAN. What about side effects /

WOMAN. I'm aware /

MAN. Mood swings, memory /

WOMAN. I'll decide.

MAN. Unilaterally.

WOMAN. It's perfectly legal.

MAN. It's unethical.

WOMAN. I'm objective.

MAN. Really?

WOMAN. Yes /

MAN. What about trust?

WOMAN. If I don't trust myself, how can I expect anyone else to trust me?

Scene Four

MAN. I think it would be good. For both of us.

WOMAN. Why there?

MAN. The country has kept incredibly accurate records. And the gene pool is probably the purest in the world. They've done some pioneering work on genetics already. I've already done some groundwork but /

WOMAN. What about your work here?

MAN. There's nothing to do but wait for the results. It would be good to start something new.

WOMAN. It looks beautiful.

MAN. Plenty of fresh air. Mountains, glaciers.

WOMAN. Isolated.

MAN. Peaceful. I can focus.

WOMAN. I'd be in the way.

MAN. We'd have some space.

WOMAN. Together.

MAN. There's a volcano. Just here.

WOMAN. I can't pronounce it.

MAN. Me either.

WOMAN. Ejaf. / Eyaf, Effaay…

MAN. Sounds like a disease. (*Adopts a voice*.) 'Doctor, I seem to be suffering from acute Eyfalakulljiol.'

Beat.

I think it could be good for both of us.

WOMAN. We haven't had much time together /

MAN. I know and a lot of that's been my fault /

WOMAN. I wasn't saying that /

MAN. I know but it's true. But we could spend some time together, relax, think about… /

WOMAN. What /

MAN. I don't know, the future…

WOMAN. Why does 'the future' always have such an ominous ring about it.

MAN. I just mean /

WOMAN. I know. You're right. Everything that's happened this year… /

MAN. Come with me.

WOMAN. Yes.

MAN. Yes?

WOMAN. Yes.

He kisses her.

No.

MAN. Hmm?

WOMAN. No. I'm…

MAN. What's the matter?

WOMAN. It's… I'm due…

MAN. I don't mind.

WOMAN. I do.

MAN. Okay.

WOMAN. Just a few more days.

MAN. Okay. (*Kisses her.*) Why don't we have something to celebrate. Wine.

WOMAN. Sure.

He exits into the kitchen.

I think I'll /

MAN. I'll have to go out.

WOMAN/MAN. What?

MAN. You…

WOMAN. I was going to take a bath.

MAN. Sure. I'll have to go out.

WOMAN. Why?

MAN. The wine.

WOMAN. Oh.

Beat.

MAN. Are you okay?

WOMAN. What?

Beat.

MAN. It's the fifteenth.

WOMAN. What do you mean?

MAN. It's usually… at the end.

WOMAN. What are you saying?

MAN. I'm asking if everything is okay? I'm just asking.

WOMAN. For fuck's sake.

MAN. I know it can become erratic…

WOMAN. I'm having a bath.

She gets up.

MAN. I didn't mean it like that.

Beat.

Shit.

He picks up his coat, wallet, etc. He heads to the front door.

The WOMAN *appears in the bathroom doorway. She is naked except for her bra and panties. The top of her leg and her panties are visibly stained red. She holds up her hand, the fingertips of which are spotted with blood.*

WOMAN. Happy now?

Blackout.

ACT TWO

Helgafjell

Scene One

A spacious living room. Decorated in Scandinavian style.

The MAN *is stood, a cup of coffee in his hand. The* WOMAN *stands near the door.*

WOMAN (*a little breathless*). Hi.

MAN. Hi. How was that?

WOMAN. Amazing.

MAN. How far did you go?

WOMAN. I don't know. I just ran. There's a hill we passed on the way here, with that huge tree.

MAN. A long way.

WOMAN. Over the other side, down to the beach.

MAN. The beach?

WOMAN. Black sand. It's beautiful. You have to see it.

MAN. I heard.

WOMAN. I'm going to go again tomorrow.

MAN. Careful you don't overdo it.

WOMAN. I feel great.

MAN. I told you.

WOMAN. The air tastes… God it was so cold at first, when your lungs feel like they're burning. Then, after a while it's incredible.

MAN. You should stretch.

WOMAN. Mmm. (*Does some stretches*.) You've got to come and see the beach.

MAN. Black sand.

WOMAN. And the cliffs.

MAN. I saw them.

WOMAN. When?

MAN. On the way here.

WOMAN. I don't remember.

MAN. You slept for most of it. Legend says that they were trolls. Caught in the sunlight.

WOMAN. Trolls?

MAN. I think. They turn to stone don't they?

WOMAN. Petrify.

MAN. Do you want some coffee?

WOMAN. No. I'm going to have a shower first. How is everything?

MAN. It's… fine.

WOMAN. Are you working? I'm sorry.

MAN. No. I needed to take a break.

WOMAN. I'm hungry. Shall we get something to eat?

MAN. We have… I don't know. We have plenty /

WOMAN. We could go into town.

MAN. Now?

WOMAN. We could drive.

MAN. It's half an hour there, then to come back…

WOMAN. Okay.

MAN. We can do it another day.

WOMAN. Sure.

MAN. You should take some water next time.

WOMAN. I didn't know how far I was going.

MAN. You need to keep hydrated.

WOMAN. It wasn't that far.

MAN. Still…

WOMAN. You should come. Tomorrow.

MAN. I still have work /

WOMAN. Just like going to the gym.

MAN. I know, it's just I've started working through the data, there's more than I anticipated. Some interesting results already.

WOMAN. Really?

MAN. I don't want to say too much.

WOMAN. Getting superstitious?

MAN. No.

WOMAN. Next you'll be wearing a lucky tie.

MAN. I just mean it's complicated.

WOMAN. I think I'd understand. I know I'm only a GP but /

MAN. To be honest I'm not sure I quite understand.

WOMAN. You used to talk about your work.

MAN. Honestly, I will. Did you see anyone?

WOMAN. No. (*Beat.*) Yes. On the way to the beach. A woman.

MAN. Really?

WOMAN. God, I've forgotten her name, isn't that awful… She was nice. Asked how we were settling in.

MAN. What did you say?

WOMAN. I said everything was fine.

MAN. Right.

WOMAN. I'll let you… /

MAN. Okay. Did she ask… /

WOMAN. What?

MAN. What we were doing?

WOMAN. I said you were working.

MAN. Hmm.

WOMAN. She was friendly. People are like that.

MAN. It's just /

WOMAN. It's not a secret.

MAN. No, course not. Still /

WOMAN. She said the sky will be clear tonight. We can see the
Northern Lights.

MAN. Really?

WOMAN. Won't that be amazing. I've always wanted to see it.
It looks so beautiful.

MAN. Okay.

WOMAN. We can sit outside.

MAN. Bit cold.

WOMAN. No, we'll take some vodka and wrap up and huddle
together for warmth.

MAN. Vodka and huddling.

WOMAN. It'll be nice.

MAN. It sounds idyllic.

WOMAN. They say it's the light reflected from the armour of
the Valkyries as they ride through the sky.

MAN. It's a nice image.

WOMAN. Of course we know better. Frejya!

MAN. What?

WOMAN. Frejya, that's her name.

MAN. Oh.

WOMAN. It's nice.

MAN. Yes.

WOMAN. I won't be long.

MAN. Okay.

> *Beat.*

> Just… /

WOMAN. What?

MAN. Just don't say too much.

WOMAN. I said I won't /

MAN. I know. I know.

> *She exits.*

> *He makes a note on a piece of paper.*

> *Blackout.*

Scene Two

MAN (*into phone*). Are you certain? Yes I understand that. I mean it's… Uh-huh. Yes of course, of course. What? The connection's terrible, wait. (*Walks.*) Two years? You mean two million and two years. It's incredible. No, I'll talk to Magnus, yes of course he'll understand, how could he not. Okay. Be discreet, okay. Yes, I know. I'll see you soon.

> *The* WOMAN *enters, she is wearing running gear.*

WOMAN. Hey.

> *He doesn't answer.*

Guess what, I saw the same woman again, Frejya, remember? On the hill, I was asking her about the area, guess what she told me?

> *Beat.*

Are you okay?

She goes to him.

Hey, are you…?

MAN. What?

WOMAN. What's the matter /

MAN. Just wait.

WOMAN. What's wrong /

MAN. Just…

Pause. Silence.

WOMAN. What's wrong?

MAN. Could I have a glass of water?

WOMAN. Sure.

She goes to the desk, picks up the jug, pours him a glass of water.

Here.

MAN. What day is it?

WOMAN. It's Tuesday.

MAN. Is it?

WOMAN. You're scaring me now.

MAN. What?

WOMAN. What's happened? /

MAN. I'm sorry. I'm sorry. Nothing's wrong, nothing's happened. No, that's not true. Nothing's wrong. Honestly… it's… I'm trying to remember everything… I mean to fix it all, what day was it, Tuesday, what was the weather like, what were we doing. You'd been out for a run. You came back.

WOMAN. What do you mean?

MAN. Margaret called. The last group of patients, they're coming to the end of the testing. Last twenty-four hours. Everything looks good. Touch wood.

You're right I'm becoming superstitious.

WOMAN. Wait a minute. The end of the testing. You mean, the end. Completely?

MAN. Absolutely. This is it.

WOMAN. Jesus.

MAN (*laughs*). I'm getting superstitious and you're turning to Jesus, it really is a landmark day in science.

WOMAN. So, you've done it?

MAN. I... yes.

WOMAN. Oh my God.

MAN. I can't even... begin to...

WOMAN. A cure?

MAN. A cure.

WOMAN. How long until...

MAN. I don't know, years probably.

WOMAN. But you've done it.

MAN. I'm so glad you're here. That you came. That we were here together.

WOMAN. Me too. You were right about this place.

MAN. It is beautiful. I'll miss it.

WOMAN. What do you mean?

MAN. Hmm? No I just mean /

WOMAN. You're leaving?

Beat.

MAN. Well, I have to get back, to /

WOMAN. Of course. I'm sorry. I just... it's such a shock. I didn't... straight away? /

MAN. I know. I mean I didn't expect... so soon... I can't quite believe /

WOMAN. So when are we going?

MAN. I don't... I have to speak to Magnus... and everyone...
   I'm not... plane tickets, no we need to... I'll call someone.

WOMAN. Come here.

She kisses him.

I'm so proud of you.

MAN. It wasn't just me... hundreds of others.

WOMAN. But you're the only one I care about.

Blackout.

Scene Three

Evening. The MAN *and* WOMAN *are eating.*

WOMAN. God this food is incredible.

MAN. Perhaps went a bit overboard.

WOMAN. It's a celebration.

MAN. More like a banquet.

WOMAN. A pagan feast.

MAN. That's good.

WOMAN. I'll have to ask Frejya for some recipes.

MAN. Who?

WOMAN. Frejya I told you /

MAN. The woman /

WOMAN. I met her /

MAN. Yes. Sorry.

WOMAN. I'll miss her.

MAN. I didn't realise you'd got to know her so well /

WOMAN. Not really. I just feel like I've known her a long time. Does that sound? /

MAN. No.

Beat.

I'm glad you came. I think it's been good. For both of us.

WOMAN. Hmm.

MAN. Just getting away from /

WOMAN. We're going back.

MAN. We can't stay here.

WOMAN. Why not?

MAN. Oh, come on. You know. I know it must seem like paradise, Eden. But I mean, look how that turned out.

WOMAN. It's clean, the air's clear. I can think.

MAN. You used to love the city.

WOMAN. No. I liked it for what it could give me.

MAN. It's a little dramatic.

WOMAN. I exploited it.

MAN. Exploited?

WOMAN. And then, eventually /

MAN. Alright.

WOMAN. You never liked it. You complained.

MAN. Yes, of course /

WOMAN. Trains, buses, prices, people, crime /

MAN. Alright, yes, it wasn't perfect.

WOMAN. And now?

MAN. It's still imperfect. But does that mean we just leave, abandon...

WOMAN. It will happen again.

Beat.

MAN. What happened /

WOMAN. Don't say you understand /

MAN. I /

WOMAN. You don't understand. You can't understand.

MAN. No, I realise /

WOMAN. A woman came into the surgery. She'd been on a bus, a group of men, some of them just boys, they smashed the window, tried to drag her off the bus. All the time they're shouting 'You fucking bitch' /

MAN. Listen don't upset yourself /

WOMAN. Upset?

MAN. I just don't think /

WOMAN. I'm just telling you what happened. Her hands were cut to pieces. She couldn't open the door to my office, couldn't sign her name, couldn't hold her daughter. Afterwards I… I began to look at people differently. Every scar, every cut, every burn I saw seemed like either a confession or a lie.

MAN. There's nothing wrong with feeling like that. It's natural.

WOMAN. Is it?

MAN. I mean, as a reaction.

WOMAN. I don't want it to feel normal. That's what I'm afraid of.

MAN. We could always move…

WOMAN. That's what I said.

MAN. I mean another part of the city.

WOMAN. Gated community?

MAN. Would you feel safer…?

WOMAN. Is that how we make ourselves safe, by becoming prisoners?

MAN. Are we prisoners here?

WOMAN. No.

MAN. An island?

WOMAN. It's different.

MAN. It just seems different.

WOMAN. They live differently.

MAN. Culturally yes but…

WOMAN. So we're all heading down the same road. Inevitably?

MAN. No I'm not saying that.

WOMAN. I'm sorry, I didn't mean to ruin the evening.

MAN. You haven't.

   Beat.

WOMAN. You're going to be famous.

MAN. I don't think that's something to aspire to.

WOMAN. I'm not impuning your motives. Just a side effect.
Interviews, profiles…

MAN. TV shows?

WOMAN. The Kick-boxing Molecular Biologist /

MAN. It was kung fu /

WOMAN. The papers will love it /

MAN. It was only a few lessons…

WOMAN. You were getting into it.

MAN. Just trying to stay fit.

WOMAN. C'mon, show me something.

MAN. What?

   She gets up.

WOMAN. Come on. I want to learn.

MAN. I'm not remotely qualified…

WOMAN. Just a few moves.

MAN. Someone will get hurt.

WOMAN. I'm a doctor.

MAN. So you should know better.

WOMAN. Please. Who knows? I may be out running and get attacked by Vikings.

MAN. That's not funny.

WOMAN. I'm just joking.

MAN. You should be careful when you're out.

WOMAN. There's no one around. It's completely safe here.

MAN. People are people.

WOMAN. Men, you mean.

MAN. Just... anything... I mean.

WOMAN. We're in the middle of nowhere.

MAN. Even so. What about this woman you met?

WOMAN. What Frejya? She's over forty, I think her raping-and-pillaging days are behind her.

MAN. That's not funny.

Beat.

WOMAN. No. It's not.

MAN. Alright... /

WOMAN. So show me.

MAN. Let's forget it /

WOMAN. No, come on /

MAN. Not now /

WOMAN (*jabs him*). Come on, don't be a pussy.

MAN....

WOMAN. Come on – (*Jabs.*) /

MAN. Stop it.

WOMAN (*jabs*).

> *She lunges at him. He counters and traps her arm.*

> Shit!

> *He lets go. Beat.*

MAN. Are you okay?

WOMAN. It's fine /

MAN. I'm sorry.

WOMAN. Don't worry.

MAN. I'm really sorry.

WOMAN. I asked.

MAN. Even so.

WOMAN. You should come running with me.

MAN. I /

WOMAN. You haven't done any exercise while you've been here.

MAN. I've been a little busy in case you hadn't noticed /

WOMAN. I know. You're right. But it would do you good. Get some fresh air.

MAN. Maybe.

WOMAN. What about the volcano? We were going to go walking /

MAN. Sure… /

WOMAN. Frejya told me that it's a sacred place.

MAN. I'm sure.

WOMAN. There was a village nearby. They held trials there.

MAN. Trials?

WOMAN. Witchcraft.

MAN. I see. Well, that's where superstition leads I suppose.

WOMAN. She gave me a book.

MAN. Witchfinders' handbook?

WOMAN. It's interesting.

MAN. I'm sure.

WOMAN. I thought you were interested in the history of the country.

MAN. I am, more genealogical data than anecdotal but /

WOMAN. Purity that's what you said.

MAN. Yes.

WOMAN. All those family ties, bonds of tribe, culture.

MAN. Yes.

WOMAN. And they still turned on each other.

MAN. Raised on superstition, religion, ignorance /

WOMAN. Husbands and wives accused each other.

MAN. You're in a lugubrious mood tonight.

WOMAN. Sorry.

MAN. Dark, brooding. Very Nordic. It's very attractive.

WOMAN. Really?

MAN. I may have had too much wine.

WOMAN. Or not enough. (*Refills his glass.*)

MAN. *Skol.*

WOMAN. *'Ég mun ekki skreppa frá verð sem þarf að vera greitt, Mímir.'* [I will not shrink from that which must be paid to Mimir.]

MAN. What does that mean?

She kisses him.

WOMAN. Do you like it?

MAN. I didn't realise you'd learned any of the language /

WOMAN. Just the important bits /

MAN. Really?

WOMAN. Spells and incantations.

MAN. I see /

WOMAN. Sex and death are all bound with magic /

MAN. I bet.

She kisses him.

WOMAN. *'Svá hjalpi þér*
hollar véttir,
Frigg ok Freyja
ok fleiri goð,
sem þú feldir mér
fár af höndum.'

[So may the holy ones thee help, Frigg and Freyja and
favouring gods. As thou has saved me from sorrow now.]

They begin to undress each other.

Striking light/sound change.

*Audioscape: in the dark, the sounds of sex. It becomes more
and more frenzied, at the last moment a cry in the dark.*

Scene Four

The MAN *and* WOMAN, *both dressed in outdoor gear. He is
sat at the table clutching his hand. In pain.*

*As she speaks she goes into the kitchen and comes back with a
bowl, and a small first-aid kit.*

WOMAN. Are you okay? Just hold it closed.

MAN. I'm okay. Shit.

WOMAN. Let me look. Here, give it to me. Open.

MAN. Christ it hurts.

WOMAN. Okay, it's not too deep. I'll have to sterilise it.

MAN. Alright.

WOMAN. It'll sting.

MAN. Just /

WOMAN. Alright. Hold still.

She holds his hand over the bowl. She takes a bottle of vodka.

Look at me.

Beat. She pours the vodka over his hand.

MAN. Fuck.

WOMAN. Hold on. (*Takes a bandage and dresses the wound.*) Move your fingers.

He does.

Okay, no tendon damage. It'll take a few days to heal, I'll change the bandage in a day or two. Are you okay?

MAN. Yeah, I'm fine. Thanks.

WOMAN (*pours him a glass of vodka*). Here, drink.

MAN. I don't /

WOMAN. Drink.

He drinks.

I'll make some tea.

MAN. So much for healthy outdoor pursuits.

WOMAN. I'm sorry /

MAN. I'm not angry /

WOMAN. I shouldn't have gone on ahead like that /

MAN. I was just /

WOMAN. I should have waited /

MAN. I was just taking a minute /

WOMAN. I know. I got carried away. I should have let you catch your breath /

MAN. Like I said I was just /

WOMAN. I know. It was my fault.

MAN. I wasn't saying /

WOMAN. It was. I got carried away. It can be dangerous up there.

MAN. I'm fine. It was an accident.

WOMAN (*kisses him*). I'll make the tea.

She goes into the kitchen.

MAN. It's getting colder, had you noticed?

WOMAN (*off*). I don't know. Maybe.

MAN. Winter's coming.

WOMAN (*off*). I bet it's beautiful in the winter.

MAN. Yes. I suppose. Still, would you want to be here all alone, cut off?

WOMAN (*off*). Here, people prepare.

MAN. Hmm.

She comes back in.

WOMAN. Just be a minute.

MAN. You look different.

WOMAN. What?

MAN. Healthy, strong. Out there.

WOMAN. I feel… /

MAN. I can see it, really. The change.

WOMAN. I feel good. I mean I haven't felt like this for… I don't remember.

MAN. Good.

WOMAN. In fact, there's something /

MAN. What?

WOMAN. I know, before, my periods had become irregular and /

The phone rings.

MAN. Sorry. Just let me. One second, it could be /

WOMAN. No, it's okay.

He picks up the phone.

MAN. Hello? Yes.

Beat.

No, tell me.

Blackout.

Scene Five

The MAN *and the* WOMAN. *He is pacing, in his hand is a bottle of pills, he is struggling with his bad hand to get the lid off.*

WOMAN. Call her again.

MAN. I told you /

WOMAN. Call her.

MAN. She said /

WOMAN. It's too important /

MAN. I know how important it is. It's been my life for two years /

WOMAN. I just meant /

MAN. I'm not an idiot /

WOMAN. I wasn't saying.

MAN. These fucking pills /

WOMAN. Let me /

MAN. I can do it. Shit.

WOMAN. Did she say what the symptoms were?

MAN. Briefly. Flu-like symptoms first, high temperature /

WOMAN. Well maybe /

MAN. No. Then it changed, inflammation, jaundice, blood
coagulation /

WOMAN. All of them? /

MAN. That was the first /

WOMAN. Perhaps they can still /

MAN (*throws the bottle down*). FUCK IT!

> *Pause. The* WOMAN *goes to pick up the bottle.*

Leave them, just /

WOMAN. Here.

MAN. I said leave them. Fucking hand. Christ what were you
thinking?

WOMAN. What?

MAN. Nothing.

WOMAN. Call Margaret back. Or get in touch with someone in
the field.

MAN. How many times /

WOMAN. I don't understand why /

MAN. I can't have any contact.

WOMAN. What are you talking about?

MAN. It was a condition.

WOMAN. Condition of what?

> *Pause.*

Condition of what?

MAN. The patent rights had exclusivity. The researcher is not
allowed contact with the subjects.

I can't do anything even if I wanted to.

WOMAN. Because of a contract?

MAN. Financial conflict of interest.

WOMAN. Financial /

MAN. They funded the whole programme.

WOMAN. What about the patients?

MAN. The subjects /

WOMAN. Subjects?

MAN. It was a trial.

WOMAN. What about them?

MAN. Do you think I don't care /

WOMAN. Then /

MAN. If they die then everything is finished. The last two years. Over. The cure. Gone.

WOMAN. And the subjects?

MAN. They were all fully informed. They signed the papers, we had consent. No one was misled.

WOMAN. You're worried about legalities?

MAN. Of course not.

The phone rings. They both stare at it.

WOMAN. Aren't you going to answer it?

Beat.

I said /

He picks up the phone. Switches it off.

What are you doing?

Beat.

MAN. It's over.

Blackout.

ACT THREE

Naströnd

Scene One

The WOMAN *is sat reading. Outside the weather is becoming more hostile.*

After a moment the MAN *enters, he has a hood up / hat on, jacket, gloves, etc.*

WOMAN. Where have you been?

MAN. Walking.

WOMAN. Walking, where?

MAN. The beach.

WOMAN. God, you must be freezing.

MAN. I'm fine.

WOMAN (*touches him*). You're frozen. Sit down. What were you thinking?

MAN. Just wanted…

WOMAN. Wanted what? Why didn't you tell me? Have you eaten anything? You've been gone hours.

Why didn't you tell me where you were going?

MAN. I didn't know. Just found myself there.

WOMAN. At the beach?

MAN. Stood there like a human sacrifice to the gods of fucking futility.

WOMAN. You can't give up.

MAN. You don't give up on nature, you just finally acquiesce to it.

WOMAN. You've only just started your research here /

MAN. I haven't found anything /

WOMAN. Then you keep looking.

MAN. You really do want to stay here, don't you?

WOMAN. It isn't about that. I said we should go back.

MAN. I'm not ready to face /

WOMAN. Then don't use me as an excuse.

   Beat.

   I know you're angry.

MAN. Angry? I'm not... I don't even have the words.

WOMAN. Fine. I'll let you... You should change your bandage.

MAN. 'Yes, doctor.' Any other searing medical insights you
   want to share?

WOMAN. It'll get infected if you don't.

MAN. How thrilling.

WOMAN. You're being a child /

MAN. Aw, you're hurt /

WOMAN. I'm not going to mother you.

MAN. God forbid.

WOMAN. What?

MAN. Just go.

WOMAN. What does that mean?

MAN. I didn't /

WOMAN (*hits him*). You fucking twisted shit /

MAN. Stop it /

WOMAN. You cunt /

MAN. Alright. I'm sorry. Stop it. Stop!

   *He wrestles control of her. She grabs his bandaged hand and
   squeezes.*

Agony. He lets go of her.

WOMAN. Don't you ever /

MAN (*clutching his hand*). I'm sorry.

WOMAN. Ever.

MAN. I know. I'm sorry.

She picks up her coat.

WOMAN. You'll need to see to that.

She exits.

Music. Blackout.

Scene Two

Night.

She is clearing away some bottles. He enters. She stops. Pause.

MAN. Hi.

WOMAN. Hi.

Pause.

MAN. How was /

WOMAN. I was just.

MAN. Sorry /

WOMAN. No, go on.

Beat.

Did we disturb you?

MAN. No.

WOMAN. How is it?

MAN. Going back to first principles. Non-coding DNA
    sequences. Telomeres, methylation, epigenetic effects.
    The data sets are good.

WOMAN. Pristine genes.

MAN. Almost. But I'm missing something…

WOMAN. You'll find it I'm sure. Are you okay? /

MAN. Headache. It's nothing.

WOMAN. You should relax. You haven't taken a break all week.

MAN. It's just a headache. I took some pills.

WOMAN. You need to be careful /

MAN. I am /

WOMAN. I'm serious. A staggered overdose, it can lead to kidney problems, brain damage.

MAN. I'm being careful /

WOMAN. Just watch your intake. And stop pushing yourself so hard /

MAN. I can't stop.

WOMAN. I didn't say stop. I just said /

MAN. Ninety-eight per cent of the genome doesn't code for proteins, there must be something.

WOMAN. They say people here can trace their ancestors a thousand years.

MAN. Is that what Frejya says?

WOMAN. You should have come for a drink, she's interesting /

MAN. I will /

WOMAN. I understand. Just don't want you getting cabin fever.

MAN. You know I read some of your book.

WOMAN. My book?

MAN. I mean, Freyja's book. The book she gave you.

WOMAN. Did you?

MAN. Listen to this: 'The seven condemned were taken out to the woods to a cliff above a great bonfire and pushed to their death in the fire below.'

WOMAN. Nice.

MAN. And that's after the ordeals by pain. 'The accused were forced to walk over red-hot ploughshares or hold a red-hot iron.'

WOMAN. Don't.

MAN. The wound was often bandaged and examined three days later, if the wound had healed it was proof God had intervened.' Here's another –

WOMAN. That's enough.

MAN. Spells, runes. Like a window to the past. I mean, our past. (*Taps his head.*) In here. Like one of those flight recorders. Lost for years. And then, suddenly we know why the plane vanished.

WOMAN. Do you want a drink?

MAN. No I /

WOMAN. Come on /

MAN. Okay.

She takes two glasses and brings the bottle.

WOMAN. I'll clean up in a minute.

MAN. Just you and Frejya?

WOMAN. And Gróa.

Beat.

MAN. Gróa?

WOMAN. She's a friend of Frejya's.

MAN. I see.

WOMAN. I was trying to learn some more of the language.

MAN. Did you get far?

WOMAN. Not really. They asked me to teach them some words, phrases.

MAN. Yes? /

WOMAN. Out of pity I think. She said I'd make a good teacher.

MAN. Really?

WOMAN. You don't think? /

MAN. I've never thought about it /

WOMAN. Would I?

MAN. Yeah, sure.

Beat.

Have you been thinking about it?

WOMAN. No. I don't know. Perhaps. Yes.

MAN. For how long?

WOMAN. Just thinking.

MAN. You've got a good career.

WOMAN. That's not the same as being a good doctor.

MAN. You are a good doctor.

WOMAN. Really?

MAN. Of course.

WOMAN. How can you tell?

MAN. You make good choices.

WOMAN. Like being here?

MAN. Maybe.

She pours two drinks.

WOMAN. *Skol.*

MAN. *Skol.*

WOMAN. No wait.

MAN. What?

WOMAN. What about a game?

MAN. A game?

WOMAN. Just the two of us.

MAN. Chess?

WOMAN. No, a drinking game.

MAN. I don't think /

WOMAN. It's cultural.

MAN. I see.

WOMAN. They love to drink here.

MAN. Clearly.

WOMAN. Okay, so here's what we do /

MAN. Isn't this a little juvenile /

WOMAN. Shh… I'll stand – no – you stand up – okay – so – wait – music –

She puts the stereo on.

Now, here, take a glass, wait – (*Fills his glass with vodka.*)

MAN. Hang on, how much /

WOMAN. Shh, these are the rules. Okay, you stand over there against the wall.

He does so.

And I'll go here. (*Fills her glass with vodka and goes to the opposite wall.*)

MAN. What exactly /

WOMAN. No, hush. Here – The game of the object /

MAN. The object of the game.

WOMAN. Hush, you're always correcting me.

Beat. She composes herself.

The object of the game is this. We start to walk towards each other. Every step, you take a drink.

MAN. Every /

WOMAN. Every step. And then we meet in the middle and if we're both still standing we take a drink and then spin around.

MAN. Oh God /

WOMAN. And whoever is left standing is the winner.

MAN. You don't really /

WOMAN. Yes really. Now come on. On three we start.

MAN. Can't we just /

WOMAN (*Icelandic*). One, two, three.

They begin the game. Each step, they drink. They meet. Both are unsteady.

They stand, face to face.

MAN. So now…

WOMAN. Drink.

They drink.

Go!

They spin round. They both stagger and fall.

MAN/WOMAN. Fuck – shit.

They sit laughing. Both are a little hysterical.

MAN. That's so fucking stupid.

WOMAN. I know.

Beat.

Truth or dare.

MAN. What?

WOMAN. Truth or dare? /

MAN. Oh, you're joking?

WOMAN. Tell me something /

MAN. What /

WOMAN. Anything. A secret.

MAN. What kind of /

WOMAN. Don't think, just speak.

MAN. I can't...

WOMAN. Anything.

MAN. Okay. You know something? It's true, and I don't know
how it happened but, a few months ago, back home... I was
in a shop that sold coffee machines. And as I walked around
I realised that I was looking at coffee machines in the same
way I used to look at sports cars when I was a kid. I mean
when the fuck did that happen? You know it's a terrible thing
to admit but I think if I'd stayed in there any longer I would
have gotten an erection.

They both laugh at this.

Your turn.

WOMAN (*still laughing*). Okay. Truth. (*Tries to control her
laughter.*) I think the worst thing about being gang-raped is
trying to get the come stains out of your dress.

Beat.

Your turn.

Blackout.

Scene Three

The MAN *is asleep on the couch. The* WOMAN *is sat on the
floor reading through some papers. After a moment the* MAN
wakes.

WOMAN. Hello, sleepyhead.

MAN. What time is it?

WOMAN. Seven.

MAN. In the morning?

WOMAN. Evening.

MAN. I was just resting. What are you doing?

WOMAN. Reading.

MAN. Are those mine?

WOMAN. I couldn't find my book.

Beat. The MAN *reaches behind him and pulls out her witchcraft book.*

MAN. Sorry. Are those /

WOMAN. I know I shouldn't but /

MAN. They're just notes /

WOMAN. I know.

MAN. Can I…?

WOMAN. I wasn't prying, I was bored.

MAN. No, I know. I just… not finished.

Beat. She hands his papers back to him.

WOMAN. How's your head?

MAN. It's /

WOMAN. Do you want some aspirin?

MAN. I'll get it /

WOMAN. It's fine, I'll do it.

She gets up, goes into the kitchen. He collects together his papers. She returns.

I didn't realise how much work you'd done.

MAN. It's just some notes /

WOMAN. Defensins, gene methylation.

MAN. I was trying a new avenue. I thought gene expression.

She hands him a drink.

(*Drinks.*) Jesus, what's this?

WOMAN. Hangover cure. Traditional.

MAN. Tastes like wet carpets.

WOMAN. It's no worse than those protein shakes. Drink it.

MAN. What's in it?

WOMAN. Just drink.

MAN. How did you find it? Was it what's-her-name… Frejya?

WOMAN. No, Gróa. Her mother used to make it for her father.

MAN. Is he still alive?

WOMAN. No.

MAN. I'm not surprised. (*Beat*.) I think we /

WOMAN. It's very interesting, all this – (*Indicates his papers*.)

MAN. Can we /

WOMAN. Gróa was asking me what you did.

MAN. Right, look I think, what? When? What did you say?

WOMAN. I explained a bit. As best I could.

MAN. Right.

WOMAN. Why are you so /

MAN. It's just sensitive.

WOMAN. I didn't mention the trials. I was vague.

MAN. Good. Fine. I want to talk about last night.

  Beat.

WOMAN. Okay.

  Beat.

  What do you want to talk about?

MAN. What do I want…? (*Beat*.) What do I want to talk about?

WOMAN. Are you okay?

MAN. Am I? (*Beat*.) No, no I'm not okay.

WOMAN. Then tell me /

MAN. Is it true?

WOMAN. What?

MAN. Is it true? What you said. What happened?

WOMAN. I don't know what /

MAN. Were you raped?

WOMAN. What?

MAN. Please, just tell me.

WOMAN. Was I /

MAN. Please!

WOMAN. I don't know what you're talking about.

   Beat.

MAN. Alright, just tell me, please.

WOMAN. I don't know what /

MAN. Yes or no?

WOMAN. What? /

MAN. Yes or no?

   Pause.

WOMAN. No.

MAN. Then why did you say you were?

WOMAN. I never said anything like /

MAN. Last night. Here. You said…

WOMAN. Said what?

MAN. You said. Back home, I mean when the riots… you said… did anything happen?

WOMAN. I told you, there was some trouble in the surgery, the window was smashed, some people came into the waiting room, they were looking for drugs or /

MAN. But nothing else?

WOMAN. No. Of course not.

MAN. You'd tell me.

WOMAN. Of course.

MAN. Last night.

WOMAN. Last night, you passed out.

MAN. No, before.

WOMAN. Before?

MAN. We drank, that stupid bloody game…

WOMAN. I'm sorry it was a bad idea.

MAN. No, wait a minute /

WOMAN. You're tired, you're hungover. You've been working too hard.

MAN. I'm fine.

WOMAN. Are you sure?

MAN. What do you mean?

WOMAN. Is there anything you want to talk about?

MAN. About what?

WOMAN. Work. What happened. The trials.

MAN. I can't /

WOMAN. It's like we led separate lives. I'd go to the surgery, you'd go to work /

MAN. I know it was difficult for you /

WOMAN. I'm not blaming you /

MAN. I wanted to talk to you. I do… I can't /

WOMAN. I'm not asking for facts. I want to know how you feel.

MAN. I don't think my feelings are…

WOMAN. Important?

MAN. Pertinent.

WOMAN. I just want to know.

MAN. I don't know. Loss, regret, anger, guilt. Textbook.

WOMAN. There was nothing you could have done.

MAN. No. Perhaps.

WOMAN. You couldn't have known she'd have that kind of reaction.

MAN. I know…

Pause.

What do you mean 'she'?

WOMAN. The subject.

MAN. Why would you say that?

WOMAN. I thought you said /

MAN. That information is confidential. Why would you say 'she' /

WOMAN. I didn't /

MAN. You've been going through my papers.

WOMAN. What are you talking about?

MAN. My notes, my files.

WOMAN. Why on earth would I do that?

MAN. I don't know.

WOMAN. Are you accusing me?

MAN. I'm asking you. /

WOMAN. It was just a guess. I mean it was one or the other.

MAN. No.

WOMAN. Just calm down.

MAN. Don't tell me to calm down.

WOMAN. I'm not telling, I'm asking.

MAN. How did you know?

WOMAN. I didn't.

MAN. Then why say 'she'?

WOMAN. Because you say her name.

Beat.

MAN. What?

WOMAN. In your sleep. You say her name.

MAN. I /

WOMAN. You can talk to me.

MAN. No.

WOMAN. Please, I want you to.

MAN. No, this is /

WOMAN. I want to help you.

MAN. I say her name?

WOMAN. Just sometimes. In your sleep. I hear it.

MAN. No, you can't.

WOMAN. You were sleeping /

MAN. I never knew her name. I never knew any of their names.

Beat.

WOMAN. Then who is Ania?

Blackout.

Scene Four

The WOMAN. *With her, the body of a fox.*

MAN. What is it? Is it dead?

> *Beat.*

> Is it dead?

WOMAN. Yes.

MAN. Where did it come from?

WOMAN. I brought it in.

MAN. You brought it in the house?

WOMAN. Yes.

MAN. Well, why did you... What happened? You shouldn't touch it.

WOMAN. It's dead.

MAN. Why did you bring it here?

WOMAN. I couldn't just leave it /

MAN. It could have a disease.

WOMAN. I don't think /

MAN. How do you know? Don't touch it.

WOMAN. It's alright.

MAN. What happened?

WOMAN. I found it?

MAN. Found it where?

WOMAN. Outside, in front of the house. I think /

MAN. What?

WOMAN. Maybe I hit it with the car, I don't.

MAN. Let me see.

> *He gets closer, but doesn't touch it.*

> I can't see any obvious injury.

WOMAN. We might have killed it.

MAN. I don't think so /

WOMAN. How do you know?

MAN. I don't /

WOMAN. Then what are you talking about? /

MAN. Why are you so upset?

WOMAN. It's dead.

MAN. Did you see anyone else or... /

WOMAN. What do you mean?

MAN. I don't know I just thought maybe someone /

WOMAN. What? /

MAN. I don't know maybe they're vermin, like foxes back home.

WOMAN. You think someone killed it?

MAN. No. It probably just...

   Beat.

   We should dispose of the body.

WOMAN. We can bury it.

MAN. Well... Yes, if you like.

WOMAN. I'll do it.

MAN. Do you think we need to report /

WOMAN. You said it was natural causes.

MAN. Yes. Even so.

WOMAN. Who would we tell?

MAN. I don't know.

WOMAN (*starts to cry*).

MAN. Hey, it's okay. (*Goes to her.*) It's no one's fault.

WOMAN. It's so beautiful.

MAN. It's okay.

WOMAN. I'm sorry.

MAN. There's nothing to be sorry for.

WOMAN. I /

MAN. Shh. Everything's going to be fine.

WOMAN. I'm pregnant.

Blackout.

Scene Five

The MAN *and the* WOMAN. *He has a testing kit, hypodermic, etc.*

WOMAN. No.

MAN. Just let me /

WOMAN. No /

MAN. It's for your own good.

WOMAN. Don't tell me that.

MAN. You're a doctor.

WOMAN. So don't try and tell me my job /

MAN. I'm not /

WOMAN. I'll drive into town.

MAN. Is there even a pharmacy?

WOMAN. Then I'll find one.

MAN. The weather is terrible, driving's dangerous /

WOMAN. I'll manage.

MAN. But we have everything we need here. Stop being so stubborn.

He takes her arm, she breaks free.

WOMAN. I've told you I don't want you to.

MAN. It's just a blood test.

WOMAN. I can wait.

MAN. We need to know. To plan, to talk.

WOMAN. Talk?

MAN. Don't you think?

WOMAN. Discuss options.

MAN. If you want to put it like that.

WOMAN. Why now. Why this minute?

MAN. Why wait?

WOMAN. What are you afraid of?

MAN. I just want to be sure.

WOMAN. Sure of what?

MAN. For God's sake, it's just a little blood.

WOMAN. Then it can wait.

MAN. Fine. You want to wait.

WOMAN. Just a little.

MAN. Then we wait. Never mind that it's blowing a gale outside. That we have nowhere to go. Ignore the fact that we have perfectly good equipment here to do the test. Forget all that. We'll wait.

He rubs his head.

WOMAN. What's wrong?

MAN. Nothing. My eye.

Another spasm of pain.

WOMAN. What's the matter?

MAN. Christ. It's just a headache. My glasses, I was working without them.

WOMAN. You need to be careful.

MAN (*in pain*). It'll pass. It's just… Fuck.

WOMAN. I'll get you something.

MAN. No. It'll be fine.

WOMAN. Don't be silly. It could be serious /

MAN. I'm not… It's just fucking eye strain /

WOMAN. Or a brain tumour /

MAN. Christ, is this your bedside manner?

WOMAN. I'm sure it's not a tumour. Just be careful.

MAN. I am /

WOMAN. You're working yourself too hard /

MAN. It's nothing to do with /

WOMAN. You're getting yourself worked up.

MAN. Then let me do the bloody test.

Beat.

WOMAN. Will it make you happy?

MAN. Don't you want to know?

WOMAN. Why don't you just ask me?

MAN. Ask you what?

WOMAN. It wouldn't matter though, would it. You can't take my word for it. Empiricist, even in love.

MAN. I don't know what you're talking about.

WOMAN. It's yours.

Beat.

MAN. That was never /

WOMAN. Yes it was.

MAN. No.

WOMAN. You want to know if there's a cuckoo in the nest.

MAN. A blood test will – (*The pain returns.*) /

WOMAN. What? Give you peace of mind? Why don't you believe me?

MAN. I didn't say that.

WOMAN. Then what?

MAN. Afterwards.

WOMAN. Afterwards?

MAN. You were distant, I mean we barely slept together.

WOMAN. That's not true.

MAN. Yes it is.

WOMAN. And what is that, an admission?

MAN. It's a common indicator.

WOMAN. So unless we're constantly fucking I'm suffering from rape trauma?

MAN. I mean the timing /

WOMAN. It was a bad time.

MAN. Yes.

WOMAN. I told you /

MAN. What happened. Yes. You did.

WOMAN. And?

MAN. I saw the surgery afterwards. A broken window you said /

WOMAN. I told you some people came in looking /

MAN. Men? /

WOMAN. Looking for drugs. There was a fight in the waiting room /

MAN. A fight? /

WOMAN. Not even that just… shouting, they were trying to frighten people /

MAN. It was a group?

WOMAN. No, not… more than one. Is that a group?

MAN. What did they say?

WOMAN. I told you?

MAN. They calmly asked for drugs? /

WOMAN. I said they were shouting. We told them we didn't have what they wanted /

MAN. You said that?

WOMAN. Sarah told them /

MAN. And? /

WOMAN. And they just said /

MAN. Said what?

WOMAN. What difference does it make?

MAN. What did they say?

WOMAN. They said, 'I'll kick your fucking cunt in'. There. Word for word.

MAN. And what did you do?

WOMAN. What could I do? I gave them what I had.

MAN. You gave /

WOMAN. Yes. Alright. And after I handed it over one of them spat in my face and called me a stuck-up bitch. And he said if I told the police he'd tie me up, rape me and pour petrol down my throat and set me on fire. Are you satisfied now?

MAN. Why didn't you tell me?

WOMAN. Yes, why didn't we sit down and have that conversation?

MAN. I just mean /

WOMAN. Now you've got your confession.

MAN. That's not what I wanted.

WOMAN. No?

MAN. No.

WOMAN. You wanted proof.

MAN. No. /

WOMAN. Science demands /

MAN. That's not it /

WOMAN. Really?

MAN. Yes.

Beat.

WOMAN. It would be a long time before you really knew, wouldn't it?

MAN. What?

WOMAN. Years. You'd have to keep checking: does it resemble me? Does it act like me? Does it have my traits, my character? Like watching an experiment.

MAN. I'd know eventually.

WOMAN. Yes, but think of the cost, the effort, all that expenditure to raise someone else's child.

MAN. Well thanks to science those questions need no longer pertain.

Beat.

WOMAN. You know it could be a chimera growing in there.

MAN. Chimeras are very rare.

WOMAN. Not unheard of though.

MAN. No.

WOMAN. A DNA test proving beyond a shadow of a doubt that a woman wasn't related to her own children. Until it was later proved that she was.

MAN. People with two sets of DNA are an anomoly.

WOMAN. Two different blood types in the same person.

MAN (*pain*). Again, it's rare /

WOMAN. Not like I'm claiming immaculate conception.

MAN. No.

WOMAN. Just nature.

MAN. Exactly.

WOMAN. Without God, what is damnation?

MAN (*pain*). What is that supposed to mean?

WOMAN. We don't know what's lurking deep in there, do we?

MAN. Where? /

WOMAN. Our reptilian history coiled up inside us /

MAN. What do you mean /

WOMAN. Sleeping.

MAN. What is? /

WOMAN. We're all children of the dark /

MAN (*pain*). Fuck…

WOMAN. Savages.

> *The* MAN *clutches his head in pain. She goes to him and puts her hands on his head. She whispers something to herself. After a moment she takes her hands away. He looks up.*
>
> *Blackout.*

Scene Six

The MAN *is sat at the table. He has a glass of water. He is studying some papers. After a moment the* WOMAN *enters.*

WOMAN. I buried it.

MAN. Hmm? Oh… yes. Good.

WOMAN. What are you reading?

MAN. Nothing /

WOMAN. Secrets?

MAN. No.

WOMAN. Let me see /

MAN. Really /

WOMAN. You've gotten so secretive.

MAN. I /

WOMAN. Maybe you always were I just hadn't noticed.

MAN. I don't think so /

WOMAN. More difficult to hide it here.

MAN. Are you going out today?

WOMAN. Trying to get rid of me?

MAN. That isn't what I meant.

WOMAN. I was going to go for a walk.

MAN. Not running?

WOMAN. No /

MAN. Because /

WOMAN. The baby would be fine.

MAN. Of course. Maybe I'll come.

> *Beat.*

> Or not.

WOMAN. No, it wasn't /

MAN. Unless you're meeting someone.

WOMAN. Someone?

MAN. Frejya, Gróa?

WOMAN. No, I hadn't planned to.

MAN. Then /

WOMAN. I thought I'd go alone.

MAN. I see.

WOMAN. I just need /

MAN. Sure. Where did you bury it?

WOMAN. Hmm? Oh. Behind the house.

MAN. I was doing some reading. There's a strain of rabies.
   Arctic rabies. The Arctic fox is the main host.

WOMAN. Really /

MAN. Apparently so.

   Beat.

   You said when you found it, it was already dead?

WOMAN. Yes.

MAN. Uh-huh.

WOMAN. I wasn't bitten.

MAN. No. Good.

WOMAN. I would have said /

MAN. Sure /

WOMAN. I'm not stupid, or reckless.

MAN. I know. I know. Of course.

   Beat.

   But saliva, it's possible /

WOMAN. I'm not infected.

MAN. It was dark /

WOMAN. I was careful /

MAN. I'm just saying it's deadly.

WOMAN. I know what rabies /

MAN. I mean we don't know how it died, how long it had been dead, do we?

WOMAN. No, but /

MAN. Don't you think we should make sure?

Beat.

WOMAN. You mean a blood test?

MAN. Just a precaution.

Beat.

For Christ's sake, think about the baby. Think about yourself.

WOMAN. I didn't touch it.

MAN. It was dark.

WOMAN. You don't believe me?

MAN. It's possible /

WOMAN. You think I'd risk the baby?

MAN. No.

WOMAN. I wouldn't.

MAN. Then why don't we make sure?

WOMAN. You want to make sure?

MAN. It's a simple test /

WOMAN. I can drive to the capital.

MAN. It's two hours away, when the roads are good.

WOMAN. I'll go slowly.

MAN. I'll drive you.

WOMAN. I can drive myself /

MAN. Then I'll go with you.

WOMAN. You don't need to, maybe some time apart would be /

MAN. What do you mean?

WOMAN. I could spend a few days.

MAN. And stay where?

WOMAN. Find a hotel.

MAN. Alone?

WOMAN. What?

MAN. No.

WOMAN. Excuse me?

MAN. I don't want you to /

WOMAN. Really?

MAN. It's not what /

WOMAN. Why not?

MAN. Listen /

WOMAN. You think I'm driving all that way for /

MAN. No.

WOMAN. To fuck someone.

MAN. It's only two hours.

Beat.

WOMAN. Fuck you.

MAN. I didn't mean it /

WOMAN. Fuck off.

MAN. Bad joke.

WOMAN. Is that what you think?

MAN. Of course not.

WOMAN. They why say it?

MAN. I don't know /

WOMAN. What's wrong with you?

MAN. What?

WOMAN. At first I thought it was because of what happened with the trials. I could understand that /

MAN. There's nothing /

WOMAN. Then you started work again. I thought it was a good thing /

MAN. It was, you encouraged me to /

WOMAN. And then when I told you about the baby you changed.

MAN. No.

WOMAN. Yes you did. You can't see it.

MAN. This has nothing to do with the baby.

WOMAN. Doesn't it?

MAN. You think I don't want a child?

WOMAN. Do you?

MAN. Of course I do.

WOMAN. Then what? /

MAN. I've been threatened.

Beat.

WOMAN. What?

MAN. I've had threats. Not just me. I got a phone call the lab back home had been broken in to.

WOMAN. A phone call?

MAN. Yesterday, Margaret phoned. Someone broke in, smashed some equipment, graffiti /

WOMAN. Why didn't you tell me?

MAN. There was nothing to tell. These things happen. It could have just been vandalism.

WOMAN. But you don't think so?

MAN. I don't know. Maybe just coincidence. I received some emails.

WOMAN. What kind of emails? /

MAN. The usual. Protesting the trials, all sorts of outrageous claims. These things happen.

WOMAN. Why didn't you tell me?

MAN. I didn't want to worry you. Besides there may have been nothing to it.

WOMAN. Is that what you believe?

MAN. I don't know. But there have been instances. It's not unknown. Anti-vivisectionists, pro-life groups. These things can turn violent.

WOMAN. But not here?

MAN. There are groups all over the world. Everyone's connected.

WOMAN. You think we're in danger?

MAN. No. I'm sure it was just an isolated incident.

WOMAN. You don't think they'd hurt anyone?

MAN. Usually no. But /

WOMAN. It's in our nature.

MAN. These acts are to create awareness not terrorise people.

WOMAN. Usually.

MAN. We're safe.

WOMAN. Could they find us?

Beat.

MAN. No.

Beat.

Who have you spoken to?

WOMAN. What?

MAN. About what I do here?

WOMAN. You think? /

MAN. I'm just asking.

WOMAN. No one.

MAN. You told Frejya.

WOMAN. Yes but /

MAN. She knows.

WOMAN. No. Nothing really.

MAN. And Gróa?

WOMAN. Are you serious?

MAN. I'm asking you /

WOMAN. You don't really believe that they'd be connected to /

MAN. People talk. Word spreads.

WOMAN. You can't just accuse /

MAN. I'm not /

WOMAN. I've said nothing. Nothing that could be misconstrued. What are you afraid of?

MAN. I told you /

WOMAN. No. What are you really afraid of?

MAN. What?

WOMAN. If someone came here. To harm us. Me. To hurt us.

MAN. I told you that's such a remote possibility /

WOMAN. We're all alone here.

MAN. We're safe.

WOMAN. Could you protect us, if it came to that?

MAN. It won't.

WOMAN. Could you?

MAN. I... /

WOMAN. Back home, before we came here, a man was cycling home. A group of men stopped him. They pulled him off his bike, kicked him, beat him. Then they stabbed him in the face. They filmed it all. And then just walked away. That happened three streets from where we live.

MAN. That was different. Rioting. It was an aberration.

WOMAN. You're so naive.

MAN. I'm what?

WOMAN. They could kill us.

MAN. No one is going to /

WOMAN. They'd rape me.

MAN. Stop it.

WOMAN. It happens. All the time.

MAN. Not here.

WOMAN. It's just like anywhere else. That's what you said.

MAN. We're safe.

WOMAN. Are you going to defend us? /

MAN. For God's sake /

WOMAN. Defend the homestead, me, yourself? When have you had to defend anything besides your reputation?

MAN. Nothing is going to happen /

WOMAN. You'd fight them off? Kill them?

MAN. You're being ridiculous.

WOMAN. Am I?

MAN. No one's going to have to fight anyone, I told you, these people /

WOMAN. When was the last time you fought someone. The school playground?

MAN. What are you saying?

WOMAN. I'm asking if you could keep us safe.

MAN. These people don't want to kill anyone.

WOMAN. How do you know?

MAN. Because that's not their agenda. They want to draw attention to what they see as medical mispractice. You know the narrative.

WOMAN. But you're helping people.

MAN. They don't see it that way.

WOMAN. Helping mankind.

MAN. Well, they have their reasons /

WOMAN. Your methods?

MAN. I don't know.

WOMAN. Your methods are sound?

MAN. Yes.

WOMAN. Ethical? /

MAN. Absolutely.

WOMAN. Then why you?

MAN. I don't know.

WOMAN. Truth or dare?

MAN. What?

WOMAN. Who is Ania?

MAN. For God's sake /

WOMAN. Why you?

MAN. I don't know /

WOMAN. You're lying.

MAN. This is absurd.

He pushes past her.

WOMAN. Where are you going?

MAN (*the pain in his eye returns*). Out.

WOMAN. Out where?

MAN. I don't know /

WOMAN. You said yourself, it's not safe.

MAN (*extreme pain*). Fuck! Jesus!

WOMAN. What's the matter?

MAN. Fucking eye.

WOMAN. I'll get you some pills.

MAN. Christ.

She picks up some pills.

WOMAN (*holds them*). Why you?

MAN. Why do you keep /

WOMAN. Why you?

MAN. I don't know – (*Extreme pain.*) /

WOMAN. Tell me /

MAN. Just give me the fucking pills /

WOMAN (*takes up the bottle, tips some of the pills onto the floor*).

MAN. What the fuck are you doing?

WOMAN. They think you're guilty?

MAN. I don't /

WOMAN. Of what?

MAN. I don't know, please /

WOMAN. Of what /

MAN (*extreme pain*). I –

Beat.

WOMAN. What?

MAN. They must have spoken to someone /

WOMAN. About what? /

MAN. What difference does it /

WOMAN. About what? /

MAN. Everything was working /

WOMAN. The trials? /

MAN. Early results were good. We'd focused on stage zero of the disease. Easily detectable variations. We were optimistic. I wanted to go further.

WOMAN. What do you mean /

MAN. Not just me, there were discussions, very frank discussions /

WOMAN. What do you mean 'further'?

MAN. You have to try and understand /

WOMAN. You jeopardised the trials?

MAN. No /

WOMAN. Someone pressured you? /

MAN. We were trying to save lives. Millions of lives. You're a doctor /

WOMAN. So are you.

MAN. We ease suffering /

WOMAN. Not at any cost /

MAN. We had to make a choice, was there a risk? Yes. But it was a calculated risk.

WOMAN. Calculated?

MAN. I, we decided to be bolder. Help more people. Even people in the late stages, everything showed we could arrest the spread, repair the damage.

WOMAN. But you couldn't.

MAN. The late-stage mutations were too aggressive. What if it was someone you loved, waiting, being eaten away, day by day what would you do? Evolution has brought us to the

point where we can control it. Should we use that power.
Should we accept our inheritance or relinquish it.

WOMAN. Who was Ania?

MAN. No one /

WOMAN. Don't lie to me /

MAN. Ania was the name we gave to the project.

Beat.

Could I have those pills now, please?

She hands him them. He swallows.

WOMAN. In the morning I'm going to drive to the capital.

Beat.

Are you listening?

MAN. Fine.

Beat.

WOMAN. You should have stopped it. Why didn't you?

MAN. I mistook hope for vanity.

Blackout.

Scene Seven

The MAN *and the* WOMAN.

WOMAN. We should call someone.

MAN. Who?

WOMAN. I don't know.

MAN. I'll take a look.

WOMAN. I'm telling you /

MAN. I know.

WOMAN. I tried /

MAN. I'll take a look. See if I can get it started.

WOMAN. You don't know anything about engines.

MAN. It can't hurt /

WOMAN. You might make it worse /

MAN. It's just an engine, I'm sure I can /

WOMAN. It was running fine.

MAN. And now it isn't, it happens /

WOMAN. I just mean /

MAN. What?

WOMAN. We need to get it fixed.

MAN. I'm not arguing with you /

WOMAN. What if it was deliberate?

MAN. What?

WOMAN. What if someone /

MAN. Don't get carried away /

WOMAN. You said /

MAN. You're jumping to conclusions.

WOMAN. Do you want to wait for proof? We're alone out here.

MAN. We're not in danger /

WOMAN. They broke in to the lab /

MAN. That's different /

WOMAN. Doctors have been killed before /

MAN. That's a specific agenda /

WOMAN. Bombings, arson, shootings.

Beat.

Magnus will have a number for the breakdown services. I'll
call him.

WOMAN. Good – Today?

MAN. I don't. / Yes.

WOMAN. Now?

MAN. Fine.

WOMAN. We should have left before winter came.

MAN. You wanted to stay.

WOMAN. You were working.

Beat.

MAN. You need to start thinking about the baby.

WOMAN. Is that what you're doing?

MAN. Yes.

WOMAN. Yes. Because it's part of you.

MAN. I didn't mean that.

WOMAN. It's true. Genetically the baby's closer to you than
    I am.

MAN. Nothing is going to happen. To you or the baby. You
    need to stay calm. Okay?

WOMAN. I know.

MAN. I just mean.

WOMAN. I know. I remember. Do you?

MAN. Yes.

WOMAN. No you don't. Because you've never felt real fear.
    That's what fetal distress feels like. Absolute helpless terror.

MAN. I /

WOMAN. No, you don't know. You don't understand. You
    know the words but when it comes to pain and fear and love
    we are a breed apart.

MAN. I'm sorry I wasn't there for you.

WOMAN. It was your child too.

MAN. I know.

WOMAN. But you could still be so indifferent.

MAN. It wasn't that.

WOMAN. No?

MAN. Not indifference.

WOMAN. I could feel it dying.

MAN. I'm sorry.

WOMAN. So don't you ever accuse me of not caring.

MAN. No.

Beat.

WOMAN. I fucking hate needles.

MAN. I know you do.

Beat.

WOMAN (*nods*). Let's get it over with.

He gets the kit.

Just, be careful.

MAN. Don't worry I've done this a thousand times.

WOMAN. Talk.

MAN. About what?

WOMAN. Anything. Make small talk.

MAN. You once said small talk is like morphine for a wooden limb.

WOMAN. Thank you.

MAN. Wasn't so bad.

WOMAN. When will you... /

MAN. I can start right away.

WOMAN. Okay.

Beat.

And you'll call Magnus?

MAN. Of course.

WOMAN. I mean I don't want to be giving birth on the living-room floor.

MAN. No?

WOMAN. I'm serious.

MAN. Very primal.

WOMAN. Very painful.

MAN. Aren't there some traditional Nordic birthing techniques?

WOMAN. I'll ask Frejya.

Beat.

MAN. Have you spoken to her? /

WOMAN. What?

MAN. About the baby?

WOMAN. I. Yes.

MAN. When?

WOMAN. It came up.

MAN. I thought you hadn't seen her for a few days.

WOMAN. We ran into each other at the garage.

MAN. Mmm. At the garage. Filling up the car /

WOMAN. Yes, remember /

MAN. And how exactly did children come up?

WOMAN. We were talking… what are you trying to say?

MAN. Nothing /

WOMAN. I'm sorry. I should have waited.

MAN. It's fine.

WOMAN. I was exited.

MAN. Don't worry.

WOMAN. No more secrets.

She kisses him.

MAN. I'll get started.

Blackout.

ACT FOUR

Yggdrasil

Scene One

He is sat drinking at the table. She enters.

Beat.

WOMAN. Are you okay?

MAN. Hmmm?

WOMAN. Are you /

MAN. I'm fine.

> *Beat.*

> You must have been up early. Didn't hear you.

WOMAN. I went for a walk.

MAN. How far this time?

WOMAN. I don't know. Did Magnus call? Or the mechanic?

MAN. No, not yet. Probably later. Reception isn't great.

WOMAN. It's getting worse out there.

MAN. Looks it. I'll email him later.

> *Beat.*

> Is everything okay?

WOMAN. How is the research going?

MAN. Good.

WOMAN. Diet you said?

MAN. Yes.

WOMAN. Sounds like a departure for you.

MAN. You'd be surprised.

WOMAN. Really?

MAN. Inherited conditions due to diet, diabetes /

WOMAN. A cure?

MAN. Perhaps a more effective treatment.

WOMAN. Clinical trials?

MAN. A long way off. I'm still collating.

WOMAN. I see.

Beat.

MAN. Are you hungry? /

WOMAN. I'm fine /

MAN. I could make something, whatever you like.

WOMAN. So you'll carry on?

MAN. I'm sorry?

WOMAN. Back home, you'll carry on with your research?

MAN. Yes, not sure what I'll find but /

WOMAN. Back to the lab?

MAN. Yes. If this is about staying here /

WOMAN. No. /

MAN. Then? /

WOMAN. Don't you like it here?

MAN. Of course.

WOMAN. You were so eager to come here.

MAN. I know. I'm glad we did. Facilities are great, and it's a
    beautiful country.

WOMAN. We were going to climb up volcanoes.

MAN. I know I've been /

WOMAN. Walk across glaciers /

MAN. We still can.

WOMAN. Winter's coming.

MAN. There's still time.

WOMAN. The baby will be here before long.

MAN. About that. I need to talk to you /

WOMAN. You're not worried are you?

MAN. Worried?

WOMAN. About going back?

MAN. Why would I be worried? /

WOMAN. I thought perhaps… the trials /

MAN. I told you /

WOMAN. You told me they went wrong /

MAN. The results failed to reach their primary endpoint /

WOMAN. Wasn't there an investigation? /

MAN. Of course /

WOMAN. And? /

MAN. They've yet to publish their findings.

WOMAN. I see /

MAN. Look, there's something we need to discuss /

WOMAN. So coming here wasn't an escape?

MAN. What?

WOMAN. You weren't running away?

MAN. Away from what? /

WOMAN. You never really told me what happened /

MAN. I told you as much as I can, more probably /

WOMAN. Why was your lab broken in to?

MAN. What? We've been through this /

WOMAN. Tell me again /

MAN. Why?

Beat.

WOMAN (*takes out an envelope*).

MAN. What's that?

Beat.

What is that?

WOMAN. Open it.

He opens the envelope. Takes out several pictures.

Pause.

MAN. Where did you get this?

WOMAN. I found it.

MAN. You found it, where?

WOMAN. Here.

MAN. What do you mean? /

WOMAN. It was on the doorstep when I came back.

MAN. What?

WOMAN. Someone left it here.

MAN. That's impossible.

WOMAN. Why didn't you tell me /

MAN. Where did you get this? /

WOMAN. Are they from the trials? /

MAN. There's no way anyone could have access /

WOMAN. Was that afterwards?

MAN (*looks out of the window/door, etc*). Did you see anyone?

WOMAN. No /

MAN. Are you sure? /

WOMAN. What happened to them?

MAN. We should call the police.

WOMAN. And say what?

MAN. What do you mean? /

WOMAN. Is that afterwards? /

MAN. Are you sure you didn't see anyone? /

WOMAN. I don't think so /

MAN. You don't think /

WOMAN. Who sent them?

MAN. I've no idea /

WOMAN. Someone on the team?

MAN. No. Why would they…

　　Beat.

WOMAN. You never told me /

MAN. I told you /

WOMAN. No, not really. Not the details.

MAN. Is that what you want?

WOMAN. You said there were side effects.

MAN. Yes.

WOMAN. On how many subjects?

MAN. I…

WOMAN. One? Five? Ten?

MAN. Only four were terminal…

WOMAN. But how many altogether?

MAN. The trials went on for months. You have to understand
　　by the time I realised /

WOMAN. You said not all of them died.

MAN. No.

WOMAN. Then what? /

MAN. The symptoms presented so quickly /

WOMAN. And the others?

MAN. We did everything we could /

WOMAN. They're alive? /

MAN. Yes. The ones we could help /

WOMAN. And what about the side effects, you said /

MAN. Why do you want /

WOMAN. I want to know what happened.

MAN. We got them medical care straight away.

WOMAN. Tell me.

MAN. What good can it do, you shouldn't upset /

WOMAN. Then tell me.

   Beat.

MAN. The disease is virulent, you know that.

WOMAN. I'm not asking about prognosis /

MAN. The side effects became noticeable rapidly, quicker than
   any of us could have imagined.

   In most cases before we could treat them /

WOMAN. The side effects?

MAN. Partial necrosis.

WOMAN. Affecting?

MAN. The extremities.

WOMAN. And so?

MAN. We had no choice.

WOMAN. The hands? /

MAN. We had to amputate the hands and feet.

WOMAN. How many? /

MAN. I don't /

WOMAN. Guess.

MAN. Three hundred, three hundred and fifty.

WOMAN. You amputated /

MAN. I told you there was no choice.

Beat.

WOMAN. They're all women.

Beat.

MAN. We were moving from targeted therapies to an integrated. They all had the cervical variation. It's where we started.

WOMAN. And the ones that lived. The ones you treated, are they... /

MAN. They were compensated.

WOMAN. Compensated?

MAN. Significantly.

WOMAN. And where are they now?

MAN. Back with their families... /

WOMAN. Some village, some town /

MAN. They all signed consent papers /

WOMAN. As though they had a choice.

MAN. There was never any coercion /

WOMAN. No. Not by you.

MAN. Not by anyone connected with /

WOMAN. Do you know how a good percentage of these women earn money? When they're not being guinea pigs?

MAN. They were never /

WOMAN. Surrogates. Wombs for rent.

MAN. I know. It's legal and it's profitable, I'm not saying it's right /

WOMAN. Those are the choices they have.

MAN. The women that we took… most would have gone on to
develop some variation of the disease /

WOMAN. Potentially /

MAN. They were all high-risk catergories /

WOMAN. And have they?

MAN. I don't know. We're not allowed contact afterwards.

WOMAN. I see. You were never curious?

MAN. It was a moot point.

WOMAN. Why?

Beat.

MAN. Because we had to perform hysterectomies on all of them.

Beat.

It was about keeping them alive.

WOMAN. As a moral obligation or just as a matter of good
business sense.

MAN. I'm not even going to dignify that /

WOMAN. Who performed the surgeries?

MAN. Local teams.

WOMAN. Hands, feet, wombs /

MAN. I did everything I could.

WOMAN. Yes.

MAN. I was trying to save /

WOMAN. I know.

MAN. You think I made the wrong choice?

WOMAN. You said you were sure.

MAN. I thought we could have a cure. For everyone. Would
you stop? Truly?

If you thought it was within your grasp to save millions,
change the course of human destiny? Would you stop?

WOMAN. You're right, you would have been remembered.

MAN. That wasn't why /

WOMAN. Lauded.

MAN. You think people remember the name Jonas Salk? What
matters is what he did.

I did everything I could to oversee safety, we screened
patients, handpicked medical teams.

I couldn't have done more, I'm not /

WOMAN. God? /

MAN. No.

Beat.

WOMAN. What /

MAN. Nothing /

WOMAN. Tell me.

MAN. I… /

WOMAN. What's wrong?

MAN. Sit down for a second.

WOMAN (*sits*). What's the matter?

MAN. I'm sorry. I know you hate it but I need to take another
blood sample.

WOMAN. What?

MAN. I'm really sorry. It's my fault, the sample. Your sample
became contaminated.

WOMAN. Contaminated?

MAN. I'd been working all day, I should have waited but /

WOMAN. What happened?

MAN. I made a mistake. That's what I'm saying. I'm sorry.

WOMAN. A mistake.

MAN. My head was still… I should have waited, it was late.
I just need to take another sample.

Beat.

WOMAN. What's going on?

MAN. What's going on? I just told you /

WOMAN. You made a mistake?

MAN. It could have happened to anyone.

WOMAN. Uh-huh.

MAN. Look, we'll do it now /

She stands.

What are you doing?

WOMAN. Have you been drinking?

MAN. No?

WOMAN (*the bottle*). Really?

MAN. I thought you might want one before we /

WOMAN. I don't understand /

MAN. I told you, I need another /

WOMAN. I don't want to.

MAN. Look, I understand /

WOMAN. We'll wait.

MAN. We've been through this.

WOMAN. Tell me what's going on.

MAN. I just told you /

WOMAN. No.

MAN. Excuse me?

WOMAN. What's wrong?

MAN. Nothing /

WOMAN. Is it the baby?

Beat.

MAN. I just need another blood sample.

WOMAN. Is it the baby?

MAN. I need to be sure, just run some more tests /

WOMAN. Tests for what?

MAN. I'm not sure /

WOMAN. What do you mean you're not sure?

MAN. Look, let's just /

WOMAN. Get the fuck away from me.

MAN. Calm down.

WOMAN. You're drunk.

MAN. No, I'm not.

WOMAN. Put that fucking needle down.

MAN. Okay. Okay. Here – (*Puts down the kit.*) It's down.

WOMAN. Tell me /

MAN. Okay.

Pause.

There's suggestion of a genetic abnormality.

WOMAN. What kind of abnormality?

MAN. I don't know yet. It seems to be a random base pair
insertion.

WOMAN. A genetic defect.

MAN. Yes.

WOMAN. Exactly what kind? /

MAN. Like I said. I don't know yet.

WOMAN. You don't know what it is?

MAN. No.

WOMAN. Then how do you even know /

MAN. That's why I want to run more tests.

He gently takes hold of her.

It's going to be okay.

WOMAN (*starts to struggle*). Let go of me.

MAN. It's okay /

WOMAN (*more violent*). Let go of me.

MAN (*holds*). Listen to me /

WOMAN (*pushes*). Get off me.

MAN (*grips*). Just listen.

WOMAN. Keep your fucking hands off me I know what this is about.

MAN. Don't be /

WOMAN. You can't let it go, can you?

MAN. It has nothing to do with… / did you hear what I said?

WOMAN. So convenient /

MAN. You think I'm… what? Making this up?

WOMAN. I expect you'd be glad if it wasn't yours.

MAN. What?

WOMAN. You never wanted a child.

MAN. That's not true.

WOMAN. The expense, the time, the effect on your career /

MAN. I never said anything /

WOMAN. You never would, you're a coward.

MAN. Is that right? /

WOMAN. You must have been relieved when the last one died.

MAN. You're being hysterical.

WOMAN. Is that a diagnosis?

MAN. Are you even concerned?

WOMAN. Why was the lab broken in to?

MAN. I told you /

WOMAN. Why would someone do that, why you?

MAN. Is this what it's come to? Paranoid conspiracy theories, break-ins, cover-ups?

WOMAN. Hysterical and paranoid, you do like to label, don't you?

MAN. You're acting erratically /

WOMAN. Don't try and play that game with me. I've got just as many words.

MAN. I'm not playing games /

WOMAN. Combative, anxious, prone to drinking, sleeplessness, low libido, erectile disfunction, anger /

MAN. Are you finished? /

WOMAN. Narcissistic personality disorder /

MAN. Go on.

WOMAN. Low testosterone, feels a lack of masculinity /

MAN. Brilliant.

WOMAN. Overcompensates. Lifts weights, takes classes so he can punch and kick and fight and feel like a man.

MAN. Good, let's have all the clichés, shall we? /

WOMAN. Why is it so important for you to feel what it's like to destroy?

MAN. When you've finished with the pocketbook psychology /

WOMAN. I'm finished.

She picks up her coat.

MAN. What are you doing?

WOMAN. I'm going to Frejya's.

MAN. Did you understand any of what I said /

WOMAN. I heard you say you're not sure, you're concerned, you want to take more tests.

MAN. That's right /

WOMAN. What's happened to you?

MAN. What is that supposed /

WOMAN. Who are you now?

MAN. Who am I? /

WOMAN. Look at the pattern.

MAN. What pattern /

WOMAN. It's confirmation bias. You're seeing what you want to.

MAN. What?

WOMAN. I know you've been under a lot of pressure /

MAN. Wait a minute /

WOMAN. The trials, the move. And then the headaches /

MAN. For God's sake there's nothing wrong with me /

WOMAN. I don't think you're in a position to /

MAN. I said I'm fine /

WOMAN. So you don't trust me?

MAN. It's not a question of /

WOMAN. I'm a doctor /

MAN. This is ridiculous /

WOMAN. Is it?

MAN. Yes.

WOMAN. You're never wrong?

MAN. That's not what I said.

WOMAN. It's hubris and it's already killed /

MAN. That was a controlled environment, things go wrong /

WOMAN. With you in control.

Beat.

But maybe that's what this was supposed to be.

MAN. Meaning what? /

WOMAN. What happens when you can't control it?

MAN. Think about the baby.

WOMAN. That's what I'm doing /

MAN. Sit down. You shouldn't get upset.

WOMAN. Don't try to fucking handle me.

MAN. I'm not. I'm just saying let's sit down.

WOMAN. I don't want to /

MAN. You can't /

WOMAN. Get out of my way /

MAN. Just listen /

WOMAN. Get out of the way or /

MAN. How can you be so fucking stupid?

Beat.

WOMAN. That took longer than I expected.

MAN. Please, just /

WOMAN. I'm going.

MAN. Where? /

WOMAN. I told you /

MAN. Listen to me, you've been under a lot of stress.

WOMAN. Fuck you.

MAN. Okay. Fine. Frejya. Gróa. Call them.

Beat.

WOMAN. I don't /

MAN. I'll call, give me the number /

WOMAN. What are you talking about? /

MAN. You don't know the number?

WOMAN. I'll drive /

MAN. Where?

WOMAN. What?

MAN. Frejya, Gróa…

WOMAN. What about them?

MAN. They're characters in Norse mythology.

Beat.

WOMAN. What?

MAN. Frejya, Gróa, goddesses from Nordic tradition /

WOMAN. No. /

MAN. I should have stopped this sooner /

WOMAN. What are you talking about?

MAN. I'd hoped you'd get better.

WOMAN. You're not making any sense /

MAN. Please /

WOMAN. You think I imagined them?

MAN. We've been up here all alone /

WOMAN. You think they're a figment /

MAN. I know this is difficult /

WOMAN. No /

MAN. You've been through a traumatic incident /

WOMAN. You think I'm delusional? /

MAN. You're upset /

WOMAN. They've been right here in this house.

MAN. Really?

WOMAN. Yes /

MAN. The other night I came up here. You'd been drinking /

WOMAN. No, Frejya was here, she and Gróa /

MAN. There was only one glass, don't you remember?

WOMAN. No, I… / I cleared them away… /

MAN. What she told you about the island.

WOMAN. Yes /

MAN. It all came from the books you've been reading.

WOMAN. No /

MAN. You've done this before, remember?

   Beat.

WOMAN. That was different /

MAN. After the baby /

WOMAN. That was different /

MAN. You used to talk to him /

WOMAN. No – Yes but – that was grief – I was /

MAN. In pain I know.

WOMAN. Yes.

MAN. I'm sorry. For everything /

WOMAN. No, don't /

MAN. I let you down.

WOMAN. I don't want to remember /

MAN. It's okay… now I'm here.

WOMAN. No.

He moves to her and gently, takes hold of her.

MAN. You're safe.

WOMAN. What happened in the surgery /

MAN. It's okay /

WOMAN. We'd ceased to be human. They laughed, spat,
taunted us. Told us what they wanted to do to us. The worst
thing was I know what happens to the human body. I'd spent
years learning; 'the breaking point of bone, the tensile
strength of human skin', 'what sulfuric acid does to soft
tissue'. The floor was covered in broken glass but they made
us kneel down. I looked over at Sarah. And I was so scared.
And I remember thinking, just for a second: 'Let them hate
her more than they hate me. Let them hurt her instead of me.'
And when they'd gone, afterwards, when we alone, I felt so
ashamed, so guilty.

*During the speech he slowly, almost imperceptibly, lets go of
her. Pause.*

MAN. You've no reason to feel guilty.

WOMAN. That's what makes it such a perfect evil.

Beat.

His phone rings. He takes it out.

MAN. It's Magnus. (*Answers it.*) Hello? (*Beat.*) Hello? (*Beat.*)
Yes, wait.

(*To her.*) Just give me a second.

*She walks around the apartment. She takes a book from the
table. She opens it and flicks through it. She is about to close
it when something catches her eye. She stops.*

(*Into phone.*) Just about… yes… yes we're both okay. She's
fine. Good. That's great, thank you.

That was Magnus, he said he's sending someone to get the
car fixed. Should be a few hours.

Beat.

Are you okay?

Pause. She holds up the book.

WOMAN. Witchcraft.

MAN. Yes.

WOMAN. It was with your books.

MAN. I told you I was interested, actually there's /

WOMAN (*reads*). 'It was claimed witches were able to cause impotence, cause disease in animals and people, and "slay infants yet in the mother's womb".'

MAN. It's a little gruesome.

WOMAN. You've made notes.

MAN. I was looking for any events that could help /

WOMAN. 'Pincers were heated until red-hot and then used to tear flesh off the breasts.'

MAN. Why don't I explain /

WOMAN. Why don't I remember?

MAN. Remember?

WOMAN. The book. Why don't I remember?

MAN. You started taking those antidepressants, you were self-medicating.

WOMAN. I was careful about the dosage /

MAN. I know this is difficult /

WOMAN. But it's mine?

MAN. Yes. I told you /

WOMAN. You're sure?

MAN. There's no other explanation.

WOMAN. Then why is her name inside?

Beat.

MAN. What?

WOMAN. Who were you talking to?

MAN. Magnus, I told you.

WOMAN. Why have I never met him?

MAN. What? He's been working abroad.

WOMAN. And he invited you here?

MAN. Yes. Of course.

WOMAN. I want to speak to him.

MAN. What? Why?

WOMAN. Does he know about the trials? About what happened?

MAN. Of course /

WOMAN. And he let you continue to work? /

MAN. I told you /

WOMAN. No /

MAN. Just calm down /

WOMAN. No, what does this have to do with your work /

MAN. If you just calm down I'll explain /

WOMAN. Explain /

MAN. First just calm down /

WOMAN. Don't tell me to fucking calm /

MAN. You're being irrational /

WOMAN. Get the fuck away from me /

MAN. Fine – (*Backs away.*)

WOMAN. You marked these pages in the book.

MAN. What?

WOMAN. Torture, forced confessions, witch trials.

MAN. You don't understand /

WOMAN. Why would you do that?

MAN. I told you /

WOMAN. Part of your research?

MAN. Yes.

WOMAN. Listen to me, you're not thinking clearly /

MAN. I'm perfectly clear, if you'll just listen /

She makes for the door.

(*Goes after her.*) What are you doing?

He grabs her and slams the door.

Just listen to me!

She bites him.

Fuck.

He slaps her across the face.

A moment of shock as he realises what he's done.

Wait.

She runs for the door.

He goes after her but she is too fast.

Wait!

The wind rises. A storm approaching.

He stands holding his bloody ear.

Blackout.

Scene Two

The apartment. But now in a state of disarray.

Books/papers, other items, hypodermic needle, etc., over the floor. Furniture moved.

The MAN *is sat on the floor. After a pause the* WOMAN *enters.*

She stands in the doorway and surveys the room. She enters slowly and stands opposite the MAN.

WOMAN. How long have you been like this?

MAN. Like this? This is who I am.

WOMAN. You've been drinking.

MAN. It's a custom.

WOMAN (*surveying the mess*). What is all this?

MAN. Spells, incantations,

WOMAN. Is this – (*Picks some papers up.*) This is your research, results, test data /

MAN. Meaningless /

WOMAN. This is months of /

MAN. Futility /

WOMAN. What have you been doing?

MAN. Reflecting. Digging deep into the question.

WOMAN. What question?

MAN. The only question that matters. What is a man? Stripped down to his bare components. Peel away the philosopher, the king, scientist, mystic, slave, what is he?

   Beat.

   A savage immortal /

WOMAN. I drove to the capital /

MAN. Ahh…

WOMAN. I would have come sooner, the roads were bad /

MAN. Ice /

WOMAN. Are you listening?

MAN. 'Some say the world will end in fire, some say ice.'

WOMAN. I went to the hospital /

MAN. I've been doing some research. Look, it's fascinating.
(*Pours some salt onto her arm*.) Salt, harmless /

WOMAN. I don't /

MAN. Wait.

He takes an ice cube and places it over the salt on her arm.

WOMAN. What is this /

MAN. Ice, again, completely harmless /

WOMAN. What are you doing? /

MAN. Two completely harmless substances.

Beat.

WOMAN (*discomfort*). I can feel it… / it's.

MAN. Yes?

WOMAN (*pain*). It's burning.

MAN. Wait / (*Grips her arm*.)

WOMAN (*greater pain*). Let go, it hurts.

MAN. Not yet /

WOMAN (*extreme pain*). Let go of me. (*Rips her hand free*.)

Massages her wrist.

Are you fucking insane. Are you sick?

There's a scar. There's a fucking scar.

MAN. You can keep it. Remind you of me.

She slaps him across the face.

WOMAN. Have you lost your mind, do you know how that feels?

He reveals a huge scar.

Oh my God.

MAN. 'Ecce Homo.'

WOMAN. What have you done?

MAN. Did you know the last people executed for witchcraft on the island were men?

WOMAN. Sit still /

MAN. It's true. Ironic.

WOMAN. You need to have this dressed. Sit down.

He sits, she examines the scarring.

MAN. Of course by that point, hundreds, thousands of women had gone to their deaths.

WOMAN. It's started to blister. (*Picks up the first-aid kit.*)

MAN. By then the damage had been done.

WOMAN (*rubs some cream into the scar*). Listen to me /

MAN. No, you don't understand, do you? That's what I was looking at.

WOMAN. What are you talking about?

MAN. They burned women alive to rid the world of evil but they cursed themselves, you see.

Beat. She stops rubbing the cream in.

WOMAN. I drove to the capital. I had a test. The baby's fine.

Beat.

Did you hear me?

The MAN *laughs.*

What are you laughing at?

MAN. The baby?

WOMAN. I had a scan everything's normal.

MAN. Normal /

WOMAN. Don't you see. You were wrong. The baby's healthy.

MAN. Is that what they told you?

WOMAN. I had a test, the doctor said everything was fine. Are you listening to me?

MAN. It wasn't the baby. It was you.

Beat.

WOMAN. What?

MAN. You're the one with the mutation.

WOMAN. What are you talking about?

MAN. How many?

How many have you lost?

Beat.

WOMAN. How many what?

MAN. How many children?

WOMAN. What?

MAN. Miscarriages. Early in the fetal development. Easily mistaken for heavy menstrual bleeding /

WOMAN. I've never had /

MAN. No? Think. Erratic cycle, it started after the riots, remember /

WOMAN. That was stress, you said yourself /

MAN. No. It was the beginning.

WOMAN. Beginning of what?

MAN. It's called the Medea gene. You can see why.

WOMAN. You're not making any sense /

MAN. Until now it's only been seen in fruit flies. *Drosophilia Melanogaster.*

WOMAN. What has /

MAN. Three-quarters of all known human diseases have a
recognisable match in the flies' genome. Did you know that.
We're this close.

The Medea gene selects the sex of each offspring. It selects.
Do you see. It chooses. It aborts at will.

WOMAN. Aborts?

MAN. Intergenomic conflict. Mass exterminations, with the cell
as the killing field.

WOMAN. Are you saying that I deliberately /

MAN. Evolution is pressure and change. Adaptation. We've done
so well. Become so resiliant to so much. But it's not over.

WOMAN. How?

MAN. I'd gone looking. Down in the junk. In the depths of all
that twisted, useless code. All those genes waiting to be
expressed. Like so many lights, turned off since the dawn of
creation. And now… click!

WOMAN. It's not possible /

MAN. It's a girl, isn't it?

Beat.

WOMAN. How did… /

MAN. The others were males, that's why you aborted them.

WOMAN. No, I couldn't have /

MAN. You didn't know. Not then.

WOMAN. How /

MAN. Pressure. The gene will do anything to survive. Our
brains override our genes and so our genes adapt.

WOMAN. That's impossible.

MAN. No /

WOMAN. Are you saying I can't control it? /

MAN. No, I'm saying you can.

Beat.

WOMAN. You knew it was a girl.

MAN. And your daughter will have daughters.

WOMAN. No, you knew, you did the test.

MAN. She'll carry the gene.

WOMAN. You can't know that.

MAN. Genetic defect passed through the maternal line.

WOMAN. You can't know how it will affect people.

MAN. It's her inheritance.

WOMAN. This is all conjecture. You have no proof. You knew it was girl. You did the test.

MAN. Do you want to see the results. Come to the lab.

Beat.

WOMAN. No.

MAN. You need to make a decision.

WOMAN. Decision about /

MAN. Nearly all gene mutations are harmful. It could manifest in any number of ways /

WOMAN. Then it would die out.

MAN. You'd be causing unnecessary suffering to the child. Think about the consequences /

WOMAN. You want to kill it.

MAN. I'm saying we need to consider all the ramifications /

WOMAN. No.

MAN. If you were the carrier of a disease /

WOMAN. This isn't the same /

MAN. No? /

WOMAN. Shut up. Just stop.

MAN. You're running out of time.

WOMAN. This can't be /

MAN. It has the potential to decimate the species.

Pause.

WOMAN. Part of the species.

MAN. What?

WOMAN. Pressure. That's what you said.

Two thousand years of slaughter, rape, slavery, arbitrary violence. Isn't that why? Two thousand years of pressure. So, the gene adapts.

MAN. You think this is about balancing the scale?

WOMAN. You're afraid.

MAN. You need to think beyond /

WOMAN. No.

MAN. No?

WOMAN. You can't know any of this. Not for sure.

MAN. I have the test results /

WOMAN. Just like before.

MAN. You can see for yourself.

She starts to exit.

Where are you going?

WOMAN. You need help /

He pins her against the door.

MAN. You can't just walk away from this.

WOMAN (*relents*). Okay. Just, let go. I'm sorry.

He releases her. They separate.

We need to think.

MAN. Okay.

WOMAN. We have a few weeks. We need to go back.

MAN. Fine.

WOMAN. I'd like to see the results.

MAN. Of course.

They start to exit. The WOMAN *grabs the hypodermic needle and stabs him. He recoils. She runs. He pins her down. The* WOMAN *cries out. He picks up the hypodermic and stabs her in the groin. She drops to the floor, bleeding. The wind picks up. A banging at the door. Louder. It spreads to the walls. Seemingly shaking the entire building. He goes to the door.*

Who's there? (*Suddenly he backs away from the doorway.*) What do you want? What do you want?

Suddenly he is seized. A noose is thrown around his neck.

Hooks sunk into his body. The flesh on his arms, legs and chest is ripped and stretched as he is hoisted into the air. He hangs, suspended in unbearable agony. Wounds tear, blood runs down his arms, legs and chest.

Glass shatters, screams, crashes, a howl of pain. A fire breaks out, spreading rapidly it swallows everything in an almighty conflagration.

Blackout.

Epilogue

Summer. A park. Birdsong. The WOMAN.

WOMAN (*on telephone*). The weather's changing. It's getting
warmer. I love the summers here.

I was hoping you'd come and visit, if you had time, we'd
love to see you. It seems like such a long time ago. I'm fine,
adapting, if that's the right word. Yes, I spoke to them again.
I said I couldn't tell them any more than I already had. I
don't think they'll call again. But I'm happy now. At least,
for the time being. I know I made the right decision. A new
life. He once said that 'All of us are born with the blueprint
for immortality. That's what makes it so tantalising.' I think
it was his way of saying, 'Where there is life, there is hope.'

Yes, I hope so.

*She ends the call, puts her phone away. Checks her watch.
Stands up.*

(*Calls.*) Stulka! Stulka!

*A group of girls run to her. They gather around her,
chattering and laughing.*

*She embraces the group. Smiles. The sound of female voices
as:*

Blackout.

End.

A Nick Hern Book

Valhalla first published in Great Britain in 2015 as a paperback original by Nick Hern Books Limited, The Glasshouse, 49a Goldhawk Road, London W12 8QP, in association with Theatre503, London

Cover image by Adam Loxley

Designed and typeset by Nick Hern Books, London
Printed in the UK by Mimeo Ltd, Huntingdon, Cambridgeshire PE29 6XX

A CIP catalogue record for this book is available from the British Library

ISBN   978 1 84842 497 5

www.nickhernbooks.co.uk

facebook.com/nickhernbooks

twitter.com/nickhernbooks